Strength in Weakness

STRENGTH
—IN—
WEAKNESS

H. STEPHEN SHOEMAKER

BROADMAN PRESS
Nashville, Tennessee

ISBN: 0-8054-6948-6
Dewey Decimal Classification: 253
Subject Heading: MINISTERS // MINISTRY // CHRISTIAN LIFE
Library of Congress Catalog Card Number: 88-38233

Printed in the United States of America

Unless otherwise indicated, Scripture quotations are from the Revised Standard Version of the Bible, copyrighted 1946, 1952, © 1971, 1973. Scripture quotations marked (KJV) are from the King James Version of the Bible. Scripture quotations marked (Moffatt) are from *The Bible: a New Translation* by James A. R. Moffatt. Copyright © 1935 by Harper and Row, Publishers, Inc. Used by permission. Scripture quotations marked (NASB) are from the *New American Standard Bible*. Copyright © The Lockman Foundation, 1960, 1962, 1963, 1968, 1971, 1972, 1973, 1975, 1977. Used by permission. Scripture quotations marked (NEB) are from *The New English Bible*. Copyright © The Delegates of the Oxford University Press and the Syndics of the Cambridge University Press, 1961, 1970. Reprinted by permission.

The lines from "i thank You God for this most amazing" are reprinted from XAIPE by E. E. Cummings, Edited by George James Firmage, by permission of Liveright Publishing Corporation. Copyright 1950 by E. E. Cummings. Copyright © 1979, 1978, 1973 by Nancy T. Andrews. Copyright © 1979, 1973 by George James Firmage.

Reprinted from *Chinese Architecture* by Aleda Shirley, © 1986 the University of Georgia Press.

Library of Congress Cataloging-in-Publication Data

Shoemaker, H. Stephen.
    Strength in weakness / H. Stephen Shoemaker.
      p.   cm.
    ISBN 0-8054-6948-6
    1. Bible. N.T. Corinthians, 2nd—Criticism, interpretation, etc.
2. Pastoral theology—Biblical teaching.   3. Paul, the Apostle,
Saint—Contributions in pastoral theology. I. Title.
BS2675.2.S52   1989
227'.306—dc19

                                      88-38233
                                      CIP

To Crescent Hill Baptist Church

Who honors my weakness
and
calls out my strengths

And who is willing to enter
the common weeping
as we walk in faith toward
the common rejoicing

With gratitude for our
koinonia eis to euangelion
partnership in the gospel

Preface

Father Damien was the famous "leper priest" who went to minister in a leper colony and himself caught leprosy. He tells of the profound turning point in this ministry when he stopped saying "you lepers" and began saying "we lepers." The ministry of Jesus Christ is ministry of "we lepers" because we follow him who became one with us and bore in his body our sickness. It is now the ministry we carry on in his name, for by miracle of God's mercy we have the treasure of the gospel in our earthen vessels.

The dominant pictures of the apostle Paul are of Paul the *theologian* writing doctrine or of Paul the *missionary* starting churches or of Paul the *polemist* engaged in hot theological debate or of Paul the *pastor* presiding over church conflict. But there is another Paul, Paul the *poet* who sings of suffering redeemed in Christ. In 2 Corinthians Paul sings of Christ's sufferings redeeming our suffering, of Christ's passion which has become the passion of the world and of the passion of the world which is becoming the passion of Christ. *Strength in Weakness* is the name of the song. It is his gospel. In this letter he also battles the false apostles who have invaded the Corinthian church, challenged his apostleship, and offered quite a different gospel. Against these super-apostles Paul offers the vision of the suffering apostolate. What is at stake is the authenticity of his apostleship, the shape of the gospel, and the nature of the church and her apostolic ministry.

This book, then, is a lyrical commentary, which seeks to be a theological re-presentation of the letter both in form and content. It is thus a new form of expository commentary, a "post-liberal" exposition, making use of modern scholarship and trying above all to re-present the themes and motifs of the letter. It searches first of all for the "literal" meaning of the text[1]—what Paul meant and what the words in their various structures and contexts mean—and for the song that lifts the words beyond themselves to Jesus Christ, crucified Messiah and risen Lord. If it is true to the letter, then, this book will be both a song of suffering transformed by grace and a theology of ministry arising out of Paul's controversy with the super-apostles.

Any book is the result of many gifts. I express thanks to my professor, J. Louis Martyn who, in a formative time of my life at Union Theological Seminary in New York City, taught me to read the New Testament lovingly, accurately, and discerningly as part of a holy conversation with God and God's church. I also thank Rhonda Slaton, my superb secretary, who has patiently and efficiently typed and re-typed my manuscript, then typed it over again. Thanks to Sharon Smith who helped my rusty French in the translation of Collange's important commentary. I thank my family of faith, Crescent Hill Baptist Church, who for the past seven years has nurtured my pastoral and theological vocation, who granted sabbatical time which has made it possible for me to finish this project, and who has taught me through all our common paths the truth of Paul's gospel—grace sufficient and strength made perfect in weakness. No congregation could love a pastor more, no congregation I've known lives as close to both laughter and tears and is as willing to share in the "common weeping" as we walk in faith toward the "common rejoicing." This book is dedicated to Crescent Hill.

Final thanks goes to my family, Cherrie, David, and Ann, who know my weakness and strength as no one else and who are as baffled as I how weakness is strength and strength is weakness and how grace somehow works in all.

Note

1. Raymond E. Brown defines the literal sense of Scripture as: "the sense which the human author directly intended and which his words convey." See "Hermeneutics," *The Jerome Biblical Commentary* (New Jersey: Prentice-Hall, Inc., 1968), p. 607.

Contents

Introduction

In one of the great English spiritual classics, *The Country Parson,* George Herbert, the famous pastor/poet, wrote of this letter:

> What an admirable Epistle is the second to the Corinthians? how full of affections? he joys, and he is sorry, he grieves, and he glories, never was there such care of a flock expressed, save in the great shepherd of the fold, who first shed tears over *Jerusalem,* and afterwards blood.[1]

Second Corinthians is a poignantly personal letter in which Paul defends the authenticity of his apostleship, the true shape of the gospel, and the true character of the church's apostolic ministry. Paul's opponents have focused their attacks on *Paul,* and in response, Paul at alternate moments awkward, passionate, and eloquent writes a letter which is his most self-revealing but which at the same time offers some of the most profound and exquisite glimpses of the gospel in all his letters. It is amazing what we can do under stress!

This is one of the most important of Paul's letters, but curiously one of the most neglected. Only of late has it begun to be given the scholarly attention it deserves. I am pleased to add this book to the new hearing the church is giving the letter. Second Corinthians may be undergoing a *kairos* in terms of its hearing in the church, and it is particularly needed at this time in the life of the church in America.

Call this book a lyrical commentary on 2 Corinthians, or maybe better, "Theme and Variations Upon Paul's Second Epistle to the Corinthians." It seeks to re-present the theological themes, its paradoxical and polemical motifs and its pain-honed spiritual wisdom, which fill the letter in an "embarrassment of riches." As I write this introduction, I hear the strains of Bach's magnificent *B Minor Mass*. As the orchestra and choir join to confess the Apostles Creed,

"I believe in one God,
the Father Almighty
Maker of heaven and earth. . . ."

it is as if I am hearing it for the first time, and I find the old historical faith of the church arising in me new, green as a leaf. Since my early training as a cellist, musical analogies come easy and run deep. Allow a beginning analogy.

Picture the Bible as a great manuscript of music. The human composers heard the most glorious sounds and sought to put on paper what they heard. It is the music of God played by thousands of people over thousands of years, preserved in the Holy Manuscript. The majestic overture begins with the single line, "In the beginning God created. . . ." There is the telling of old stories truer than any others ever told, there is the strong, sure metered voice of the Law, and the psalmist's full range of praise and exultation, lament and desolation, thanksgiving, lament and love song, surely, as John Calvin called the Psalms, "an anatomy of all parts of the soul." There is the homey wisdom of sages, prophet's vision and discomforting warning, and the gospel's glad tidings of great joy for all people—God's coming among us bone of our bone, flesh of our flesh, heart of our hearts. There are the early accounts of the fledgling church, epistles, and finally apocalypse, the unveiling of God's final triumph, an astonishing finale, surely an "ode to joy."

Biblical scholars are called to hard and loving labor to work over the manuscript, making sure every note is as accurate as we can humanly determine and explaining to us who live hundreds, thousands of years later what the original composers may have meant by the markings in the text.[2] We are deeply indebted to these "musicologists" of holy Scripture.

The preacher, on the other hand, is called to *sing* the music. The preacher must live with the manuscript, listen to its music, and learn it as an act of holy love. Then the preacher may re-present its beauty and truth through all the notes and themes and songs found there. The preacher who listens closely to the music and pays attention to all the markings in the manuscript knows when to be loud and when to be soft, when to laugh and when to cry, when to comfort and when to confront, when to sing and when to instruct. Some sermons are a minuet, others are a march. Some use soft strings, others use trumpeting brass. There is no freedom more wonderful than serving a biblical text and becoming its instrument.

We become servants of the actual notes of the music never believing (secretly or openly) that we can substitute better ones. However, using all the faith, courage, and imagination given us, we try to re-present the original music in musical forms that may find the ears of modern listeners, helping them to hear themes they have forgotten or never really heard. The great biblical themes and motifs remain primary, and we serve them by offering them in new musical settings to a world hungry for their sound.

I write as a preacher indebted to scholars. I can better sing because of their work. As a theological re-presentation of 2 Corinthians, this book seeks to re-present the provocative and passionate motifs of the letter in a new setting so to help us hear it better and feel its truth and pain-honed beauty.

This book is at points song and at other points working studies of the manuscript, but it is mostly song. Its beauty and truth are cruciform, like Reynolds Price's description of the voice of Maria Callas, "the dark draught of pain and ecstatic wisdom that seeped from Callas like blood from a pierced hand."[3]

Sometimes Paul is a theologian, at times a polemist, fiercely and brilliantly so when under attack; at times he is pastor presiding over congregational conflict; but there are also moments when he is "a kind of poet."[4] And never is he more a poet than when he sings of Christ and suffering. Paul turns poet when he contemplates Christ's suffering and when he sees that suffering working its holy redemption in the midst of our suffering. Our sufferings are the soul sufferings of guilt and fear, the body sufferings of disease and weakness, the world sufferings of a creation "groaning in travail" awaiting the redemption of the children of God and a kingdom coming in peace, righteousness, and joy. Christ's suffering and ours turn Paul into a poet of redemption. Karl Plank perceptively identified the "Poetic Paul and the Language of Affliction."[5] This Paul singing hymns of the cross and blacklike spirituals which hope in the redemption to come is a Paul not ordinarily seen. We tend to focus on Paul the theologian, Paul the polemist, Paul the pastor. But there is the poetic Paul, and nowhere is there a more poignant presentation of this Paul than in 2 Corinthians.

Appropriately, then, this book takes a kind of musical form, a lyrical commentary. Think of a composer who writes a symphony based upon the music of an earlier composer, like Brahm's *Variations on a Theme by Haydn* or Charles Ive's *Second Symphony* recalling many American folk tunes. Better yet, think of Bach writing the *St. Matthew Passion*. He took Matthew's voice and made him the narrator; he re-presented the words of Jesus as the living Christ speaking now; and he used well-known chorales and contemporary lyrics to voice the congregation's response. All these elements are woven into a gorgeous tapestry of music. I can still feel the emotion I first felt, though it was long ago, listening to the choir sing the Roman centurion's words, "Surely this is the Son of God." His words through the music became mine. The *St. Matthew Passion* is as profound a commentary on the Gospel of Matthew as any traditional commentary found between the pages of books.[6]

The form of this commentary will be alternately lyrical and polemical, as Paul is alternately lyrical and polemical in his stunning set of motifs. Instead of the traditional commentary form of quoting the passage then following with exegesis or exposition, I will quote from 2 Corinthians in the text itself, always capitalizing the words, phrases, and sentences, so they stand out as *leit motifs* of a symphony.

Motifs paradoxical and polemical.—This book seeks to represent the extraordinary theological motifs of 2 Corinthians, motifs paradoxical and polemical, all summed up in the single dominant motif, *strength in weakness*.

In my last reading of the Epistle, I noticed twenty-four such images/motifs: (1) comfort in suffering (1:3-7); (2) hope in despair (1:8-11); (3) yes amid the noes (1:19-20); (4) lording it over the congregation vs. serving it (1:24); (5) joy mixed with pain (2:1-4); (6) the humiliating triumph (2:14-16); (7) Spirit vs. letter (3:3); (8) light out of darkness (4:6); (9) treasure in earthen vessels (4:7); (10) life in the midst of death (4:10-13); (11) the outer vs. the inner person (4:16 *ff.*); (12) heavenly and earthly existence (5:1-10); (13) esctasy vs. sober-mindedness (5:13-14); (14) *sarx* (worldly) eyeglasses vs. *stauron* (cross-colored) eyeglasses (5:13-16); (15) the new creation in the midst of the old (5:17); (16) the suffering apostle—itself a contradiction in terms for many people ancient and modern, but for Paul an essential paradox of the gospel (6:4-10); (17) joy in the midst of grief; (18) the rich Christ who became poor (8:9-10); (19) super-apostles vs. weak apostles (chs. 10—11); (20) the false gospel of another Jesus vs. the true gospel of the historical Jesus (ch. 11); (21) boasting in the weakness (11:30); (22) strength in weakness (12:9); (23) the power of the cross of weakness (13:3-4); and (24) success in failure (13:6-9).

Such a gathering of paradoxical and polemical motifs is striking indeed. The paradoxical motifs cluster around the dominant motif: *strength in weakness*. The polemical motifs (the "versus" motifs) cluster around another motif: the super-apostle vs. the suffering apostolate. It is a conflict-laden atmosphere whose air we breathe as we read this letter. You've heard the expression, "You could cut the tension with a knife;" that's how 2 Corinthians reads.

For Paul the battle is mortal combat; the life and truth of the gospel itself is at stake, not to mention the validity of Paul's own apostleship. A false gospel of another Jesus is being foisted upon the Corinthian church. What is, therefore, at stake is the meaning of the gospel, the nature of apostleship, and the shape of the church's ministry. All through the letter Paul contends for a vision of the gospel which is summed up *"strength in weakness"* and for a definition of ministry which follows it, an apostolate willing to suffer the world's sufferings that God's grace be experienced,

willing to be weak that the power of God be made known. Therefore, this letter is not only song but also polemic. It is a defense of
the true apostolic ministry of the church, as Paul sees it, and a
definition of true apostolic ministry. (We rarely define ourselves
well until we are under attack. The most important theological
decisions of the church throughout the years have come about under the threat of theological distortion.) Accordingly this book is
not only a lyrical commentary but also a theology of ministry arising out of Paul's vision of the true apostolic ministry of the
church.

The paradoxical language of the letter is crucial inasmuch as it
corresponds to the structure of life itself and to the gospel redeeming this life. Paradox issues into polemic as the opponents of Paul
seek to foist upon the Corinthians an unparadoxical vision of life
and of the gospel, a vision which becomes either illusory (a Polly-
ana view of life) or cruel (if you suffer you are being judged). Paul
is unwilling for the gospel to be separated from suffering or for it
to be a glib answer to suffering. The mystery of suffering is held
in the mystery of the cross: a crucified Messiah raised by the
power of God to be Lord. We live in the mystery of a world being
redeemed but not yet redeemed, of a cosmos groaning in travail
awaiting its sure but future glorification.

So, in this letter we hear a music sad and sweet all at the same
time—*strength in weakness* it sings, a music ennobled and perfected in pain. And there is nothing less than mortal battle here,
the super apostles vs. the suffering apostolate—a clash of dissonance threatening to destroy the truth and beauty of the gospel, to
undermine Paul's apostleship, and to change the character of the
church.

A resolution can only come with the enduring triumph of the
paradox of the gospel which is the miracle of the cross, that love
made eloquent in suffering will at last prevail and not only prevail
but bring about the transfiguration of existence. This is in Paul's
heart the true gospel of the historical, crucified and risen Christ
who

> THOUGH HE WAS CRUCIFIED IN WEAKNESS
> LIVES BY THE POWER OF GOD (13:4).

The Stunning Pertinence of this Letter

The major theme, *strength in weakness,* and primary polemic, the super-apostles vs. the suffering apostolate, speak with stunning pertinence to us today. Life has its tragic dimension: personal suffering, a child dies of leukemia, a plane plummets to the ground taking to the grave three men long before their time, a life scarred all lifelong by the cruelty of parents, social structures rife with injustice, the random evil of disease, the calculating evil of death camps.

How does the gospel speak to the tragic realm of life? Does it enter into the "common weeping" of the world? The apostle Paul says in this letter that the gospel of Jesus Christ enters into the tragic realm of life and into our suffering. The wondrous paradox of the gospel is that in Christ there is strength in weakness, comfort in suffering, consolation in desolation, and light breaking through the darkness.

Some would offer a gospel unencumbered by history, untouched by suffering, untouchable and untouching, a gospel oblivious to life's shipwrecks and to the victims of life's bruising, battering hand. But this is not the true gospel of Jesus the Christ; this is the false gospel of another Jesus. *Strength in weakness* is a motif of the gospel relevant in every age, and Paul's paradoxical motifs speak the saving, healing truth of the gospel into the tragic realm of life.

The polemic of this letter, however, has stunning pertinance to us today, for the gospel in America is infected by a runaway success orientation. Super-apostles have invaded the American church, preaching a gospel of health, wealth, and success mixed with nationalistic American triumphalism (there is a distinction between a worthy patriotism and an unworthy nationalism). We, with Paul, must contend for the truth of the gospel. Paul refers to them as SUPER-APOSTLES, *huperlian apostolon* (11:5) and FALSE APOSTLES, *pseudapostoloi* (v. 13).

The Opponents: A Historical Excursion

The "opponents" of Paul in 2 Corinthians has been a major issue for scholars through the years. Some say that they are that superlegalistic group called Judaizers—like those whom Paul faced in Galatia. Others say that they are the overly spiritual and arrogantly wise folk we call Gnostics, who by their superior knowledge and ecstatic spiritual experience considered themselves already perfect—Paul battled these Gnostics in 1 Corinthians. Others say there were a group of Palestinian Jewish-Christians who thought themselves superior to all others. Some scholars postulate that the opponents were some combination of these; others identify more than one group of opponents.[7] A combination of external and internal evidence may be gathered to support a hypothesis concerning the opponents. I operate on the hypothesis that the opponents were of one group.

The references, direct and indirect, within the letter concerning these opponents include the following: they "lord over it" the faith of the congregation (1:24), they use letters of recommendation to bolster their authority (3:1), they boast of what is outward not what is within (5:12), they accuse Paul of preaching a gospel of death (2:15), they question Paul's relationship to Christ (10:7), they make fun of Paul's weakness in speech and appearance and of his inferiority in "knowledge" (10:10-11; 11:5-6), they accuse him of walking according to the flesh (10:2). They are skilled in the art of public speaking (11:6) and boast of coming from blue-blood Jewish stock (11:21-23). Paul, in turn, accuses them of being hucksters of the Word of God (2:17), false apostles who bring a different gospel and preach "another" Jesus (11:3-4), who pride themselves on being superior apostles with superior credentials (10:12; 11:5; 12:11). As Paul argues his points throughout the letter, we can infer that these opponents boasted of their mountaintop spiritual experiences (5:12 *ff.*; 12:1-4), of their perfection in the law of Moses and of the light of their ecstatic faces shining like the glory that shown from Moses' face (3:1-18). They probably lived and lived well off the contributions of the church. They scoffed at Paul's refusal to accept money (11:7-11) and cast aspersions on his offering for the poor in Jerusalem (perhaps accusing him out of their own guilt over milking God's people for money).

In summary, they were a group of outsiders (11:4) who went to Corinth to win the believers to their brand of Christianity. Theirs was an apostleship of power and glory (making themselves fitting heirs to James and John the sons of Zebadee who wanted to sit at Jesus' right and left hand). They exalted Moses and Jesus as super heroes whose faces shone with glory-light at Mount Sinai and the mount of transfiguration and exalted themselves as being given the same divine power. Their own faces glowed with divine light! They exalted in their strength manifest in ecstatic experience, obedience to the law, superior knowledge, and eloquent speech. And they saw success as proof of their authenticity and as proper reward for their labors. Paul's apostleship, an apostleship of "weakness," was their necessary and favorite target. Paul's gospel talked too much about the cross and suffering; moreover he himself was unimpressive in looks, speech, demonstrable spiritual experience, and results (A VEILED GOSPEL, they said he preaches).

Dieter Georgi helps us locate these opponents in the first-century world.[8] Many migrant preachers in that age went from place to place living off the contributions of the converts. Paul's opponents were such traveling missionaries of Hellenistic/Jewish background. They prided themselves in their Jewishness, propagated a "divine-man" theology (a popular religious emphasis of the times) making themselves exemplar divine-men. They gloried in their spiritual experiences and were enormously successful. As such, they would have competed well in the religious marketplace of the first-century Mediterranean world. And they would have had special appeal to Corinthians, given as this church was to fascination with spiritual fireworks and what scholars call "enthusiasm."[9] But Paul saw these SUPER-APOSTLES, these missionary miracle men, as FALSE APOSTLES promulgating a perversion of the gospel of Jesus Christ.

They find their spiritual cousins in America in the form of super-Christians, super-pastors and super-churches who promote a gospel of health, wealth, and success and who make health, wealth, and success the evidence of their spiritual authenticity. They are of varying theological stripes, but they are all into success, American style. These modern super-apostles have an advantage of Paul's opponents didn't have: modern communications, telemarketing of the gospel and computer aided solicitation. But their appeal is the same now as then: if you follow Jesus you will be healthy, successful, and wealthy—like *us*.

No letter could be more crucial for us today. The church and her ministry are in an identity crisis. Unsure of herself, the church has gone hunting cultural notions of success and cultural sources of authority. Failing to take her bearing solely from what Paul called the "truth of the gospel"—Christ incarnate, crucified, and risen—the church has frequently taken up with false gospels and false messiahs.

Second Corinthians may help us find our bearings again. As Paul makes his defense, he clarifies the true shape of the gospel and the true character of the apostolic church and her apostolic ministry. Let me define what I mean by *apostolic*.

Apostolic means being true to the vision of the New Testament church. It refers to our *message*. To be the apostolic church means to be faithful to the gospel message handed down by the first apostles. It also refers to our *mission*. To be apostolic means to be, like Paul, active in our mission to the world, sent as ambassadors of reconciliation and preaching a gospel the world hungers for but knows not.

The introduction is now through, like the introductory notes included on the record dust cover or like a conductor's introduction before a concert.[10] Now let the music begin: "Theme and Variations Upon Paul's Second Epistle to the Corinthians." We begin with an Overture which announces the main themes you will hear throughout the work. If you are anxious to get to the letter itself, you may skip to Chapter 1 and read the Overture later. If you would like to hear the major themes assembled in some kind of theological framework, proceed directly to the Overture.

Notes

1. George Herbert, *The Country Parson* (New York: Paulist Press, 1981), p. 63.
2. This analogy was aptly stated by J. F. Collange, p. 5. Throughout this book I have consulted a number of standard commentaries. I list

them now and throughout the rest of the book will reference them by the author's name only.

Barret, C. K. *The Second Epistle to the Corinthians*. New York: Harper & Row, 1973.

Beasley-Murray, G. R. "2 Corinthians" in *The Broadman Bible Commentary,* vol. 11. Nashville: Broadman Press, 1971.

Best, Ernest. "Second Corinthians" in *Interpretation* commentary series. Atlanta: John Knox Press, 1987.

Bultmann, Rudolph. *The Second Letter to the Corinthians*. Minneapolis: Augsburg, 1985.

Collange, J. F. *Enigmas De La Deuxieme Epitre De Paul Aux Corinthians*. Cambridge: The University Press, 1972.

Denny, James. "The Second Letter to the Corinthians" in *The Expositor's Bible*. New York: Funk and Wagnalls, 1900.

Filson, Floyd, "The Second Epistle to the Corinthians" in *The Interpreter's Bible,* vol. 10. New York: Abingdon Press, 1953.

Furnish, Victor Paul. "II Corinthians" in *The Anchor Bible,* vol. 32A. New York: Doubleday & Co., 1984.

Georgi, Dieter, *The Opponents of Paul in Second Corinthians*. Philadelphia: Fortress Press, 1986.

Moule, H. C. G. *The Second Epistle to the Corinthians*. Fort Washington, Penn.: Christian Literature Crusade, 1976.

Reid, James. *Interpreter's Bible,* vol. 10. New York: Abingdon Press, 1953.

Strachan, R. H. *The Second Letter to the Corinthians* in the Moffatt New Testament Commentary. New York: Harper & Brothers, 1935.

3. Reynolds Price, *A Common Room: Essays 1954-1987* (New York: Atheneum, 1987), p. 326.

4. Louis Mackey's phrase in his book *Kierkegaard: A Kind of Poet* (Philadelphia: University of Pennsylvania Press, 1971) as cited in Plank.

5. Karl A. Plank, *Paul and the Irony of Affliction* (Atlanta: Scholars Press, 1987), p. 1.

6. Paul Minear, exemplar New Testament scholar, has called Bach the most prolific biblical interpreter of the eighteenth century and provocatively (and I think correctly) calls Bach both a premodern and postliberal theologian! See these theological reflections on Bach: Paul S. Minear, *Death Set to Music* (Atlanta: John Knox Press, 1987); and his

"Bach and Today's Theologians," *Theology Today,* vol. 42, July 1985, pp. 201-210.

Jaroslav Pelikan, *Bach Among the Theologians* (Philadelphia: Fortress Press, 1986). Robin A. Leaver, *J. S. Bach as Preacher,* Church Music Pamphlet Series (St. Louis: Concordia, 1982).

7. All the commentaries listed tackle these issues. I commend especially Georgi, Furnish, and Collange.

8. Georgi.

9. See especially Ernst Kasemann, *New Testament Questions of Today* (Philadelphia: Fortress Press, 1969), p. 126; *Perspectives on Paul* (London: SCM Press, 1971), p. 123; and *Jesus Means Freedom* (Philadelphia: Fortress Press, 1969), pp. 59 *ff.* Enthusiasm believes that the kingdom has come and that we right now live in resurrection glory. The Spirit has perfected us. It is a denial of history and of the cross as the way of servant-love in history.

10. *A note on the unity of the epistle.* Scholars have debated the unity of the Epistle. Chapters 1—9 differ in tone from 10—13, the former being more optimistic in its appeal, the latter more disturbed and urgent. My judgment is that the two parts address the same issues and problems but may represent two letters with Paul having heard between the two more bad news about the progress of the super-apostles. There is some disjointedness—the reader more easily finds the conclusion of 1:1—2:13 in verses 7:5-16—and there is one fragment 6:14-7:1 that sounds like a part of another letter sent by Paul to Corinth (more in tone and theme like 1 Corinthians) which has probably been collected as part of 2 Corinthians. Paul himself refers to letters sent to Corinth which are neither in 1 or 2 Corinthians, so we may assume a number of letters sent, some of which are now missing. These observations, however, do not threaten the basic unity of the letter nor the authority of the inspiration or authorship. The letter is Paul at his most personal and Pauline. The theological themes and motifs are of the same thread and fabric, even if not woven at the same sitting.

Overture:
Main Themes Set,
Main Arguments Announced

"Life is completely fair," goes the line from "The Last Convertible," "it breaks everybody's heart."[1] Sooner or later it breaks everybody's heart. How does the gospel of Jesus Christ speak to the breaking of hearts?

A woman is about to be abandoned by her husband; a teenage boy is dumped by his first great love; a fifty-five-year-old man is out of work, victim of a corporate merger's program to eliminate older executives, and is unable to find work. Your child dies. Swindled by a business partner, your life savings is now gone. Illness has robbed your body of its vitality and beauty.

Sunday morning pews are heavy with the breaking of hearts. Call it the tragic realm of life, call it randomness or chaos or original sin. Or say it this way: "The world is too strong for us."[2] Life is completely fair; it breaks everybody's heart.

Paul's Second Letter to the Corinthians offers a word from God to us in the breaking of our hearts: MY GRACE IS SUFFICIENT FOR YOU; MY STRENGTH IS MADE PERFECT IN WEAKNESS (12:9). This letter is theme and variations upon that wonderful word: His grace sufficient.

I

If your heart has never been broken or you can never imagine it being broken, this letter is not for you. If you've never suffered, never entered into the suffering of another, or if you think you will get through life unmarked by suffering, this book is not for you.

Paul's Second Letter to the Corinthians and this book, which seeks to serve its words and its music, are based on the premises that pain and suffering are twined deeply in the structures of life itself and that being a Christian does not insulate us from this pain but rather sends us into the world of suffering as ministers of Christ. If life entails suffering, then Jesus' messiahship and our ministry in his name are bound up in life's pain.

Fred Craddock spoke in a sermon to the scandalous character of Peter's confession of Jesus as the Christ or Messiah (which is what *Christ* means).[3] The Jewish people believed, believed in great hope, that when the Messiah came there would be no more misery. When the Messiah comes, they would say, there will be no more pain, no more disease, no more babies that die, no more childless couples, and no more motherless children. When the Messiah comes, injustice will end and peace will reign; there will be no more hunger and no more war and no more death. When the Messiah comes, everything will be made right and made whole and made good. When the Messiah comes.

How incredible it is, then, that we call Jesus "the Christ" or the Messiah. Abraham Heschel, a great Jewish theologian, was conversing with his close friend and Christian theologian Reinhold Neibuhr. It was a public forum on Jewish/Christian relations. At one point Heschel characterized the difference of perspective between the two faiths this way: "to the Christian the Jew is the stubborn fellow who in the face of the coming of Jesus of Nazareth refused to call him Messiah; to the Jew the Christian is the heedless fellow who dares say the Messiah has come in an unchanged world!" While I, as a Christian, would argue his statement that the world is unchanged with the coming of Jesus, I do acknowledge the scandal of calling Jesus Messiah when the world has not been transfigured at his coming into the perfect kingdom of God.

We must acknowledge, then, that the confession of Jesus as the Christ has brought with it a completely new way of looking at the world and of looking for God. In some ways it has turned everything upside down or inside out—or maybe right side up. Fred Craddock expresses the new perspective this way: instead of saying, "Where the Messiah is, there will be no misery," we say, "Where misery is, there is the Messiah." This reversal of vision, this revisioning of our hope, is a fundamental premise of real apostolic ministry. And it is at the heart of Paul's passionate discourse in 2 Corinthians.

In this letter what is at stake is no less than Paul's apostleship, the truth of the gospel, and the nature of the church and her ministry. Super-apostles have invaded the church at Corinth, preaching the false gospel of ANOTHER JESUS (11:4). These invaders whom Paul designates FALSE APOSTLES (v. 13) parade themselves as divine-men, preach a Christ without the cross, promote a life without pain ("People are rightly suspicious," says Liston Mills, "when they are called only to joy."[4]), and create a culture-religion of super-pastors, super-Christians, and super-churches. Theirs is a kind of gospel which sold well in the Hellenistic world and which sells well today in America.

Someone has defined a heretic as a person who has a complete grasp of a half-truth. The false gospel of the super-apostles was and is dangerous because it is a half-truth parading as the whole truth. They want Messiah untouched by suffering, resurrection without the cross, and a victorious Christian life unmixed with defeat or pain. This false gospel subtly and insidiously isolates Christians from the very world "God so loved . . . that he gave his only son." If Messiah Jesus only means joy, health, wealth, and success, then Christians must deny the suffering in their lives and must avoid people who suffer.

Against the SUPER-APOSTLES who preach this false gospel, Paul offers his own gospel: (1) Jesus Christ, suffering Messiah and risen Lord; (2) calls us to be the suffering apostolate (as opposed to super-apostles); (3) who enter into the "common weeping" of the world (rather than avoiding it); (4) as "wounded healers" (as opposed to super-Christians); (5) preaching a theology of the cross (rather than a theology of glory); (6) and establishing servant-churches (as opposed to super-churches).

Jesus Christ the Suffering Messiah and Risen Lord

When Jesus came he identified with suffering folk. Inasmuch as he also rescued them from their misery, people began to call him Messiah. When he himself suffered and died, however, this served for them as a logical repudiation of his messiahship. A suffering

Messiah was a contradiction in terms. It caused cognitive dissonance. No wonder Saul of Tarsus, the fiery, brilliant, and fiercely devout Jew would reject Jesus, and no wonder he persecuted every Christian in sight.

Resurrection would have been dismissed out of hand. The Messiah could never hang "cursed from a tree," and any talk of resurrection was an idle tale. But something happened to Saul, something he could never have anticipated. On the way to Damascus "breathing threats and murder against the disciples of the Lord" (Acts 9:1), Saul saw a great light and in the midst of that light the crucified and risen Lord appeared to him. Paul later calls it an "apocalpyse" of Jesus Christ (Gal. 1:12), a revealing of Christ in glory, a resurrection appearance like those given to the disciples and apostles (1 Cor. 15:1-10).

The bright light along that road not only blinded Saul's eyes but also blinded his mind, throwing into darkness everything Saul had ever known to be true. He spent three days in physical blindness until Ananias, a Christian enemy-now-brother, was used as a vessel of healing. During three years in Arabia, Saul gradually overcame the blinding of his mind. Saul became a NEW CREATION: Paul the apostle to the Gentiles, an apostle with new eyes to see the world and a new message to preach, the gospel of Jesus Christ, the crucified Messiah who was raised by the power of God to be Lord.

This strange new gospel rearranged everything in Paul's life: how he viewed God, how he viewed the Messiah, how he viewed life's suffering, and how he looked upon his own weakness and suffering. There is a crucified Messiah and risen Lord, he cries, who is with us in our weakness and suffering who sends us to be with others in their distress, comforting them WITH THE COMFORT WITH WHICH WE OURSELVES ARE COMFORTED BY GOD (1:4). And this Lord gives us spiritual power to cope with our suffering and to grow in it until we meet the Lord face to face in the glory of heaven's perfect communion. This Christ . . .

Calls Us to Be the Suffering Apostolate

Christ does not call an elite corp of SUPER-APOSTLES, "apostles of glory" who are above suffering, untainted by human weakness, spiritual supermen who LORD IT OVER God's people as rulers. Christ calls "apostles of weakness," ordinary, flawed, suffering human beings like everyone else, who relate to God's people as SERVANTS FOR JESUS' SAKE. Inasmuch as Paul's apostleship demanded that he lead God's people, he leads as a *servant*.

Moreover, Christ's call is to the whole people of God, not just to an elite few apostles. Pentecost poured its power "on all flesh" and set all God's people menservants and maidservants to dreaming, preaching, and seeing visions. Super-apostles inevitably draw a line between themselves, spiritual giants, and the people of God. They talk of *I* (*I* saw this, did this, know this), *me* (this happened to *me*, you obey *me*), *mine* (*my* apostleship, *my* ministry, *my* church). Paul—just note as you read—speaks of *our, our* ministry, *our* calling, *our* service. WE ARE AMBASSADORS FOR CHRIST (2 Cor. 5:20). So the basic unit being called is not an elite few at the top, but is the whole people of God.

We are the suffering apostolate. In the service of the crucified and risen Lord, we minister in our weakness, acknowledging our suffering and identifying with the suffering of others. Called to be a suffering apostolate we are those people . . .

Who Enter into the "Common Weeping"

The phrase is Miguel Unamuno's, and it comes from his classic *The Tragic Sense of Life*. Listen:

> . . . I am convinced that we should solve many things if we went into the streets and uncovered our griefs, which perhaps would prove to be but one sole common grief, and joined together in beweeping them and crying aloud to the heavens and calling upon God. And this, even though God should hear us not; but He would hear us. The chiefest sanctity of a temple is that it is a place to which men go to weep in common.[5]

Compassionate ministers are willing to enter into the common weeping because they know that all griefs merge in life's one river of sorrow. Some ministers would rather stay in the superficial happiness of an illusory world, but the suffering apostolate looks at real life and is not afraid to bewail and beweep life's pain. They are unafraid to let the church be a temple where people come to weep in common.

Make no mistake. Ministry entails suffering, entering into the suffering of others and redemptive use of your own suffering. There is the suffering of love extended and not returned, the suffering of sickness and injustice and unemployment and addiction, the suffering of guilt and failure and shame. There is heartbreak all right. And to be with people in their heartbreak, to sit still and feel your own heart break, is a *sorrow*.

Compassionate ministers are able to see life's pain, listen to others' pain, and feel their own pain because they recognize that it is all part of the common weeping. Inasmuch as we can enter into this common grief, we begin the journey with God's people toward the common rejoicing.

Hope is born as people are allowed to express their hurt. When they are told to swallow their hurt, their hurt turns to despair. But when we let them voice their hurt, hurt turns to hope.[6] Biblical people are a people of hurt and hope. As we enter into the common weeping, we are given vision of the coming kingdom which is the common rejoicing. What did Jesus say? "Blessed are those who weep, for one day they shall laugh!" So, we move the through this world's common grief . . .

Ministering as Wounded Healers

Super-apostles beget super-Christians. They say that Jesus brings health, wealth, and success, and that these are signs of being blessed. As super-Christians you witness out of your strength. In this tradition today we see a train of testimonies by successful businessmen, beauty queens, sports heroes, and other famous personalities.

In 2 Corinthians Paul argues that we minister also, perhaps best, out of our WEAKNESS. God's TREASURE is in our crackable EARTHEN VESSELS, all the better for God's TRANSCENDENT POWER to shine through (4:7). Paul himself has much weakness and is tormented by the thorn in the flesh left after so many unanswered prayers. But God has told him the gospel truth: MY GRACE IS SUFFICIENT FOR YOU; FOR MY

STRENGTH IS MADE PERFECT IN WEAKNESS (12:9). Paul, and all Christ's people, minister as "wounded healers."

In his book, *The Wounded Healer,* Henri Nouwen has come up with one of the most captivating images of ministry in recent years.[7] The image comes from a story from the Jewish Talmud. Rabbi Yoshua comes to Elijah and asks, "When will the Messiah come?" Elijah replied, "Go ask him yourself." "Where is he?" asks Yoshua. "Sitting at the gate of the city . . . among the poor covered with wounds," replies Elijah, then he explains: "The others unbind all their wounds at the same time and then bind them up again. But he unbinds one at a time and binds it up again, saying to himself, 'Perhaps I shall be ready so as not to delay for a moment.' "[8]

Ministers, says Nouwen, must be such wounded healers, looking after their own wounds, wounds of loneliness, loss, sin, illness, and despair, but at the same time being available to the wounded of the world, sitting among them and caring for them in their woundedness.

Nouwen calls us not to wallow in our woundedness nor to parade our wounds in a kind of spiritual exhibitionism but rather to see our own pain and the pain of others "as rising from the depth of the human condition."[9] Our suffering is not a special case, nor is it in and of itself interesting or edifying. We see our woundedness as part of the common weeping and therefore are able to walk with the wounded of the world as ministers of Christ, bringing the saving, healing power of God to our world.

Super-apostles would promote only ministry through strength. They scorn Paul and all who minister in weakness. But Paul knows better. Wounded healers alone can carry the healing balms of God to a broken world, for to use Thorton Wilder's words, "In Love's Service only the wounded soldiers serve." Christ's true apostolate . . .

Preach a Theology of the Cross
Rather Than a Theology of Glory

This distinction was formulated by Martin Luther and has been a major way of thinking theologically since the Reformation. But nowhere is Luther more like Paul than with this distinction, and nowhere is the contrast more vividly seen than in 2 Corinthians. What did Paul say? "But we preach Christ crucified, a stumbling block to Jews and folly to Gentiles" (1:23). And Luther answered in his own century: "The cross alone is our theology."[10]

The super-apostles were theologians of glory (very much like those described by Luther[11]), glorying in their strength, their spiritual experiences, their righteousness, wisdom, and eloquence. In contrast, Paul was an "apostle of weakness." Described in the second-century *Acts of Paul* as "a man little of stature, partly bald, with crooked legs, of vigorous physique, with eyes set close together and nose somewhat crooked," and described by his opponents in Corinth as one whose BODILY PRESENCE IS WEAK AND HIS SPEECH OF NO ACCOUNT (10:10) Paul could hardly compete with these Greek-god-like apostles. Instead he gloried in the cross, the cross that gave God's forgiveness for every sin and God's strength for every weakness.

The theology of glory is the theology of super-apostles, a theology without the cross. It says that God is a God of strength who blesses his chosen with power, health, and wealth. Christ's suffering and death had its indispensable place in giving us salvation but has no place in our present way of life. In *their* formulas: Christ became human that we might become divine, Christ became poor that we might become rich, Christ became powerless that we might have power, Christ suffered that we might escape suffering.

A theology of glory trumpets the victorious Christian life and has an excessively summery spirituality largely devoid of any wintry spirituality. It thinks there is a kind of perfection we can attain now, believing—despite its protestations to the contrary—that it is by our might, wisdom, and goodness that we are saved. It thinks it gets its strength from God but in fact feeds off cultural modes of power.

In stark contrast, Paul is an apostle of weakness preaching a theology of the cross. Paul glories not in his strength but in his weakness, not in his wisdom but in the wisdom of the cross, not in his goodness but in the grace of Christ. We cannot attain salvation except through the cross. Moreover, the cross is precisely where we see the essence of God. In the cross we see and know the power and wisdom of God. Furthermore, in a theology of the cross the church is not the company of the perfect ones (whether perfect in health, wisdom, power or wealth); rather, we are, to use David Buttrick's phrase, "assuredly broken yet being-saved ecclesial communities."[12] We are being changed DEGREE BY DEGREE into Christ's likeness, but never automatically and never completely in this life.

A theology of glory is the preachment of a church which prides itself on outward signs of strength: size, wealth, wisdom, beauty, ceremony.[13] It becomes a church of, by, and for the "healthy, wealthy, and wise." In contrast, the church which preaches a theology of the cross is humble in its sense of strength, wisdom, and goodness. It is not afraid of suffering, it is unashamed of its own powerlessness, and it is a church organized for SERVICE.

These two theologies affect, then, where a church *locates* itself and its ministries—which leads to the last major theme. True apostolic churches preach a theology of the cross, . . .

And Establish Servant-Churches Rather than Super-Churches

The theology of glory is the proud posture of a church which locates itself among the "healthy, wealthy, and wise." A theology of the cross is the way of the servant-church which serves the world God so loves. Every church should ask itself: is our ministry located among the well or the sick, among the rich or the poor, among the saved or the lost, among the full or the empty, among the powerful at the center of things or among the powerless and weak on the margins of life? Then we must ask: to whom did Christ come?

While we may begin our ministry among the well, rich, saved, full, and powerful, our ministry, like that of our Lord, is always self-emptying. We follow Christ who THOUGH HE WAS RICH, YET FOR YOUR SAKE HE BECAME POOR, SO THAT BY HIS POVERTY YOU MIGHT BECOME RICH (8:9). Now we rich in grace, blessed materially and spiritually, empty ourselves in service to others. We SPEND AND ARE SPENT for the sake of others.

A super-church stays among the well, rich, saved, full, and powerful and says that its wellness, richness, savedness, fullness, and power is a sign of being blessed. A servant-church gives thanks for all it has and all it is by the grace of God, then moves to the sick, poor, lost, empty, and powerless to share from the bounty of our life and of our Lord.

The super-church is proudly self-sufficient. Gathering so many goods to itself, it feels no need for denomination or God. The servant-church needs everybody's help and finds its only sufficiency in God.

A super-church has a centripetal force sucking people and possessions to itself. A servant-church has a centrifugal force sharing people and possessions with the world. A super-church is Babel-like, building towers to God and collecting people into bigger and bigger barns. A servant-church is a Pentecost church, gifted by the Spirit and scattered all over the earth on mission.

We begin to see how much is at stake in this letter: Paul's apostleship, the shape of the true gospel, and the nature of the church and her apostolic ministry. God's church begins in the breaking of hearts and by miracle of God finds renewal of heart. We begin in weakness but end in the promise of God: MY GRACE IS SUFFICIENT FOR YOU; FOR MY STRENGTH IS MADE PERFECT IN WEAKNESS. Now to the epistle.

Notes

1. This line is from the television screenplay, *The Last Convertible*.

2. Paul Scherer, *Facts that Undergird Life* (New York: Harper & Row, 1938), p. 137.

3. Fred Craddock, *Hoping or Postponing* (New York: NCC Cassettes, 1979). From a series of sermon selections from NBC's National Radio Pulpit Series in Cooperation with the Christian Church (Disciples of Christ).

4. Cited in Karl A. Plank, *Paul and the Irony of Affliction* (Atlanta: Scholars Press, 1987), p. 11.

5. Miguel Unamuno, *The Tragic Sense of Life* (New York: Dover Publications, 1954), p. 17.

6. Walter Brueggemann, *Proclamation 3: Aids for Interpreting Lessons of the Church Year-Advent/Christmas* (Philadelphia: Fortress Press, 1984), p. 9.

7. Henri Nouwen, *The Wounded Healer: Ministry in Contemporary Society* (New York: Doubleday & Co., 1972).

8. Ibid., pp. 83-84.

9. Ibid., p. 90.

10. The distinction is most clearly made in Luther's "Heidelberg Disputation of 1518," *Luther's Works,* ed. Harold S. Grimm (Philadelphia: Muhlenberg Press, 1957), vol. 31; but you can trace it all through his writings, particularly in his "Lectures on Galatians," *Luther's Words,* ed. Jaroslav Pelikan (St. Louis: Concordia Publishing House, 1964), vol. 27; and his "Lectures on Romans," *The Library of Christian Classics: Icthus Edition,* ed. Wilhelm Pauck (Philadelphia: The Westminster Press). I am also indebted to the unpublished paper "Luther's Theology of the Cross," Robert C. Shippey, Jr., and Walther von Loewerich, *Luther's Theology of the Cross,* trans. Herbert J. A. Bauman (Belford: Christian Journals Limited, 1976). One could make the case that a theology of the cross is the key to Luther's whole theology. He himself wrote "The cross alone is our theology." *Operationes in Psalmos,* 1519-1521 in Martin Luther's Werke, 5 band, in *Weimarer Ausgobe* (Weimer: Hermann Bohlaw Nachfolgeer, 1892), p. 176.

11. "Heidelberg Disputation," p. 53. For a more complete discussion of this concept, see chap. 20.

12. David Buttrick, *Preaching Jesus Christ* (Philadelphia: Fortress Press, 1988), p. 13.

13. See Luther, "Lectures on Romans," p. 333. *The Magnificat Luther's Works, American Edition,* ed. Jaroslav Pelikan (St. Louis: Concordia Publishing House, 1956), 21:350. "The Gospel for St. Stephen's Day," *Luther's Works, American Edition,* ed. Hans Hillenbrand (Philadelphia: Fortress Press, 1974), 52:91-92.

1
The Greeting:
Grace and Peace

(1:1-3)

PAUL, AN APOSTLE OF JESUS CHRIST BY THE WILL OF GOD. (v. 1). With those words Paul begins the letter. The letter is a passionate defense of his apostleship so it is no wonder that after his name, *Paulos,* the second word of the letter is *apostolos.*

BY THE WILL OF GOD he is an apostle. Anybody who knew his story knew it wasn't by Paul's will—at least not by the outer will which controls us with its fitful willfulness, though we would hope that in his deepest, truest self Paul found himself responding with a deep willingness to the call of God. BY THE WILL OF GOD.

Paul's own will had sent him "breathing threats and murder against the disciples of the Lord" (Acts 9:1). Then it happened. Amid blinding light the risen Lord appeared and called him to be an apostle of the very One whose followers he was persecuting. Called by blinding light and amazing grace: " 'twas grace that taught my heart to fear, And grace my fears relieved." After three days and three years of preparation, Paul sensed his call to be the apostle to the Gentiles and set off across the Mediterranean world accompanied by the Spirit of God. No, the Spirit did more than accompany him, it *led* him, red light here, green light there. Luther said, "like a blinded horse" Paul was led. And wherever the gospel took Paul, it worked its holy power in people, all kinds of people. If Paul was led "like a blinded horse," he *went* because he trusted in the light that blinded him and the voice that called him and the grace that healed his very soul.

Now Paul the apostle begins his letter with the greeting—God's

people always greet each other in the Lord—GRACE AND
PEACE TO YOU FROM GOD OUR FATHER AND THE LORD
JESUS CHRIST (v. 2). Biblical people greet each other with prayers and assurances of God's saving presence that makes even this
meeting and this relationship possible. Here Paul greets us with
the two great biblical words that sum up God's blessing upon us:
GRACE and PEACE.

GRACE. God's power of love which comes *gratis,* free, as gift
(the Greek word for grace, *charis,* itself means gift), and which
is, all at the same time, the free gift of salvation, God's unconditional good pleasure in us, pardon for sin, all sins, and the power
of new life. When you hear the word *grace,* imagine God's face
lighting up with delight in you, cleansing waters flowing freely
around you, washing and refreshing. Think of words like *pardon,
power,* and *gift.*

And PEACE. The great Hebrew word *shalom* means wholeness, peace, well-being. When do you feel most whole? When you
are at peace with God, the most elemental communion. And when
you experience peace inside your own skin, and peace with the
significant others in your life. God's peace is also peace with
neighbor which extends evangelically to all nations and peoples.
We are made communal animals to live in communion; our sense
of well-being depends upon the gifts of peace which are communion and community.

In Ephesians Paul used as a metaphor of Christ's peace the
breaking down of walls, walls of guilt and hostility, of fear, misun-
derstanding, and mistrust which separate us from one another.
Peace is the breaking down of walls, the building of bridges called
reconciliation, the atonement of Christ which creates at-one-ment
with God and a healed community of persons.

GRACE and PEACE Paul greeted the Corinthians and greets
us, not the calculating grace and reluctant peace we dispense, but
the kind that comes only from God and is given freely to all who
seek it. Two words which speak to the breaking and mending of
hearts, and better still to the "renewal of the heart."[1] (Collange
repeatedly describes Paul's view of the work of Christ in the be-
liever's life as "la renovation des coeurs," the renewal of hearts.
More of this theme later.)

Will the Saints (Whoever They Are) Come Marching In?

Paul addresses the CHURCH *(ecclesia)* OF GOD AT COR-
INTH WITH ALL THE SAINTS *(hagiois)* WHO ARE IN THE
WHOLE OF ACHAIA (v. 1). Who are the saints? They are none
other than the church! The called out ones *(ecclesia)* and the holy
ones *(hagiois)* are the same. Who are the saints? Us, that's who!

You may recoil from the word *saint.* It smacks of a "holier than
thou" person, one smugly self-righteous, the kind of person that
goes around hunting for a vacancy in a stained-glass window. It is
the kind of person we associate with Pharisees, a man like John
Updike's deacon, "too much at home here"[2] in his church or like
Mark Twain's "good man in the worst sense of the word." But
such is not a biblical understanding of saint.

You may, when you think of the word, imagine those special
holy persons, singularly Christlike individuals, and to be sure
there are people like that. I love Frederick Buechner's definition
of saint in his *Wishful Thinking: A Theological ABC:* "In his holy
flirtation with the world, God occasionally drops a handkerchief.
These handkerchiefs are called saints."[3] There are such people so
transparent with the love of Christ that in seeing them you love
God all the more. But still, this is not what the New Testament
means by saints.

Nowhere in the New Testament is the word *saint* used; it is
always in the plural—the *saints!* There are no singular saints in the
New Testament, only the whole people of God, the called out
ones, those forgiven sinners so captured by the love of Christ that
they WHO LIVE, LIVE NO LONGER FOR THEMSELVES
BUT FOR HIM WHO FOR THEIR SAKE DIED AND WAS
RAISED (5:15), and thereby become *persons for others,* seeking
to love the world as God loves the world.

The holiness of the saints does not consist of moral perfection
(though it calls us to high moral standards) but of a people who
give themselves away in love. We are forgiven and freed to forget
about ourselves long enough to love somebody else.

So when you see *saints,* think plural, think, absurd as it may
seem, *you,* you as part of that company of called-out ones. Super-
apostles exalt the singular role of the *hero* (holy men, an exclusive

club). But Paul speaks of *our* ministry, our "partnership in the gospel" (*koinonia eis to euangelion,* Phil. 1:5), the shared ministry of the apostolic church. The apostolic ministry belongs to the whole church. *Baptism is every Christian's ordination.* When Paul defends his apostleship, he is defending not only himself but also the character of the ministry of the whole people of God.

So when you hear Paul's words and read the word *minister* or *ministry* in this book, what we are referring to is you, not just the professional ministry, but the shared ministry of the whole people of God.

Notes

1. Collange, p. 66.
2. John Updike, "The Deacon" in *Museums and Women and Other Stories* (Greenwich: A Fawcett Crest Book, 1973), p. 40.
3. Frederick Buechner, *Wishful Thinking: A Theological ABC* (New York: Harper & Row, 1973), p. 83.

2
The God of Comfort

(1:3-7)

"Life is completely fair; it breaks everybody's heart." To the breaking of hearts Paul offers his God, THE GOD OF ALL COMFORT WHO COMFORTS US IN ALL OUR AFFLICTIONS, SO THAT WE MAY BE ABLE TO COMFORT THOSE WHO ARE IN ANY AFFLICTIONS, WITH THE COMFORT WITH WHICH WE OURSELVES ARE COMFORTED BY GOD (1:3-4). Paul offers this God and Jesus Christ, the One whose broken heart has become the gateway to life.

Ministry begins in suffering. The grace of God is poured from broken heart to broken heart. Unbroken hearts are quite unusable for ministry; they are like shiny pottery vessels with no openings either to receive or to give the healing balms of God. For the desolation of hearts only God's consolation will finally do, a consolation brought by Christ and his servants.

Ten times in five verses we see the word *comfort*. Do you get an idea of its importance? The New Testament word is *paraklesis*. You may remember that word from some other place: Jesus talking of God sending us another paraclete, another like *him* (John 14:16 *ff.*). *Paraclete* literally means "one called *(klesis)* alongside *(para)*." Wayne Oates says that God's presence comes in two forms: as *overagainstness* (the Holy Other meeting you face to face) and as *alongsideness* (God coming to walk by your side as Friend).[1] Jesus was the supreme Paraclete of God, alongsideness made flesh, God's Son who came to earth and walked beside us as Friend.

But this friendship was a suffering friendship. Jesus was the "Suffering Servant" envisioned by the prophet, a man of sorrows and acquainted with grief, one who bore our sins and bore them away, the one whom we would despise and reject but by whose stripes we find our healing.

It is his broken heart that becomes our passage to the grace of God. He is the Christ of sorrow and comfort. I love the way H. C. G. Moule expanded on this climactic moment from Bunyan's *The Pilgrim's Progress*. Christ is the Man at the Gate:

> "Here is a poor burthened sinner," said the Pilgrim; "I would know, Sir, if you are willing to let me in."
>
> (And we would say with the pilgrim) "Here are stricken and broken hearts; we have heard, Sir, that your heart was once broken, and has stood open ever since, and that its great rift is turned into a gate by which men go in and find peace. We would know if you are willing to let us in."
>
> "I am willing with all my heart," said the Man; and with that he opened the gate.[2]

The broken heart of the Son of man has become the open gate to eternal life. It has also been the occasion of our calling into the ministry of Jesus Christ, the ministry which is not for professionals only but of the whole people of God.

Suffering and Ministry

What strange language. We back away. FOR AS WE SHARE ABUNDANTLY IN CHRIST'S SUFFERINGS, SO THROUGH CHRIST WE SHARE ABUNDANTLY IN COMFORT TOO (v. 5). Is this some pious form of masochism, some kind of sick religion that has a morbid fascination with suffering?

What does it mean to share in Christ's sufferings? Permit a definition of suffering: *suffering is being acted upon.*[3] When you are ill, disease acts upon you. When one you love rejects or abandons you, you are acted upon. It is your life at the disposal of other persons and outside forces: hatred, neglect, rejection, poverty, disease, oppression, death. Suffering is vulnerability to life and all life brings, to actions and circumstances beyond your control.

Suffering is bound up in real living. It is being acted upon by the terrors of falsehood and cruelty. It is also being acted upon by the pleasures of beauty, truth, and love, and being forever changed.

But one cannot suffer the pleasures of one without the injury of the other. We will be hurt by love and surely grow sick of love at times, but we do not have the choice of pain and no pain but rather the pain of loving or the pain of not loving. We can go outside and catch a germ, but what life is sadder than the boy who, because of no immune system, must live his whole life inside a sanitized protective bubble?

Suffering is living life vulnerable. It is being acted upon. If you live, you suffer. God has no magic protective bubble that protects us from suffering.

What, then, are "the sufferings of Christ?" Let us look at Christ, the suffering Son of man. God became the suffering God as he sent his own Son to earth to be acted upon. Christ was acted upon by creation; he got weary and tired, caught cold, and suffered the daily afflictions we all bear. He also was acted upon by other persons: misunderstood, rejected, nailed to a cross, hung in humiliation on a Roman gallows. He also gloried in creation's splendor and was loved and adored by some of his followers, but all of this was only possible by being also vulnerable to life's sufferings.

Christ also suffered by coming to this earth and voluntarily taking on the suffering of humanity. There is the "common weeping," and Christ took on our common weeping. There are storms, and Christ has endured them with us. Shakespeare's Lear speaks:

> Poor naked wretches, wheresoe'er you are,
> That bide the pelting of this pitiless storm,
> How shall your houseless heads and unfed sides,
> Your loop'd and window'd raggedness, defend you
> From seasons such as these?[4]

Christ came and identified with suffering humanity, taking on our pain and befriending especially the poor, the outcast, the sick, and the sinner.

We begin to understand the meaning of "the sufferings of Christ," then, as we observe the actual way of the Son of God in our history. And the model of the incarnation guides our discovery of how WE SHARE ABUNDANTLY IN CHRIST'S SUFFERINGS (v. 5).

They are the same two forms of suffering Christ endured: the sufferings we voluntarily take on in the service of love, and the sufferings we necessarily endure because we are human but which we lift to Christ that his Spirit may transfigure them into redemptive suffering. Suffering becomes redemptive as his grace brings into our suffering the graces of comfort and calling, deep comfort for our pain and a calling that turns us to the world to minister as "wounded healers."

Let me elaborate on these two ways of sharing in Christ's suffering. There is the suffering we voluntarily take on in the service of love. These sufferings are, I believe, the *crosses* Christ bids us to take up when we follow. The way of the Son of man in history was the way of identification with the suffering ones. We, too, walk alongside those traumatized by the world. We identify with the poor, and as we bear their suffering we become their comforters and advocates. We give voice to the voiceless, we help empower the powerless, we help bring into the family circle those marginalized by poverty, handicap, race, and idiosyncrasies. The amazing victory of the early church as it rose from a tiny, illegal sect to the dominant religion of the empire happened because it incarnated its compassion by establishing help for the poor and sick and dying, orphans, travelers, and victims of calamity.[5] Welfare for the poor, hospitals, hostels, orphanages all came into being through the early mission of the church. Throughout the centuries God's Spirit has prompted reform movements which have taken up the cause of the poor and dispossessed, for example, the Franciscans of the thirteenth century, the social gospel movement in America at the turn of the twentieth century, and the theologies arising out of the poor "base communities" of Central and South America and among oppressed minorities all over the world today. These are all expressions of sharing in Christ's sufferings.[6]

As the church, we can choose to isolate ourselves from the sufferings of the world; we can flee to suburbs and super-church structures that provide us all we "need" so we don't come into contact with the "world." We can become increasingly and exclusively white, wealthy, and American. We can identify only with the winners, the successful and healthy and beautiful. But as we isolate ourselves from the suffering ones, we abandon the Christ who leads us to them and indeed waits for us in them (Matt. 25:31-46).

So the first way we share in the sufferings of Christ is to identify voluntarily with the suffering of others. These are the crosses we are called to take up. The second way has to do with how we *meet* the sufferings that necessarily come our way because we are human. These are not crosses to bear, these are *burdens,* and Scripture has different instruction to us concerning them. Crosses we are to take up (Matt. 16:24), but as for burdens, "Cast thy burden upon the Lord, and he shall sustain thee" (Ps. 55:22, KJV).

As the sufferings of life come our way, we yield them to Christ for the ministry of his grace. Our sufferings are transfigured, that is, made redemptive, by the comfort of his presence and by the calling which thrusts us into the world as wounded healers.

We have a choice about our suffering. We can curse it and receive it totally apart from God's Spirit. This can lead only to bitterness, cynicism, and defeat. Or, we can offer it to God, praying that somehow in the midst of this bad darkness (it is bad and it is dark) that God's light can shine through, that somehow in the pain we will find our spirits enlarged, our minds deepened, our hearts softened. I do not wish to seem glib; this transfiguration is not easy or automatic or ever complete. William Sloan Coffin, in the aftermath of his son Alex's death, spoke of the terrible pain but also of the new wisdom: "Another consolation, of course, will be the learning—which better be good, given the price. But it's a fact: few of us are naturally profound; we have to be forced down"[7]

John Donne, facing a life-threatening health crisis, wrote a series of meditations. In one of them he spoke of misfortune as gold bullion that we carry on our journey, useless unless coined into currency. God's Spirit can help us face our misfortune and coin it into some useful currency. "*Tribulation* is *Treasure* in the *nature* of it, but it is not *currant money* in the use of it, except wee get nearer and nearer our home, heaven by it."[8] Unless we yield our sufferings to Christ, they more likely will become overbearing loads to haul on life's way.

So crosses are the voluntary sufferings we take on as followers

of Christ, and burdens are the necessary sufferings of life we endure and cast upon the Lord. In the mystery of God's redemptive
purpose, these two realities, crosses and burdens, coincide in
Paul's challenge to "bear one another's burdens, and so fulfil the
law of Christ" (Gal. 6:2). One person's burden becomes another
person's cross, and the church becomes the redemptive place
where we take up others' burdens and find the comfort of others
bearing ours. COMFORT WITH THE COMFORT WITH
WHICH WE HAVE BEEN COMFORTED (v. 4). This reality is
more than simple human companionship (though that is grace in
and of itself). As we share in these, *Christ's,* sufferings, we discover that we SHARE ABUNDANTLY IN COMFORT TOO, *his*
comfort.

What I am describing is the path of real life that brings us truly
alive in this life and prepares us for the feast of life to come. Jesus
Christ came in vulnerable human flesh and suffering human love
to show us how to be real.

Have you read the children's classic *The Velveteen Rabbit?* It
tells of a stuffed velveteen rabbit in a child's room which at
Christmas-time was left over in the corner when all the shiny new
mechanical toys were given as gifts and came to live in the house.
The velveteen rabbit felt lonely and rejected and quite inferior to
the new gadgets and toys in the house. One day he struck up a
conversation with the wisest and oldest toy in the house, the Skin
Horse. The Skin Horse's brown coat now was bald in patches.
Most of the hair on his tail had been pulled out, but he had seen
many shiny mechanical toys come and go, and he was still around.

The Rabbit asked the Skin Horse one day when they were lying
side by side:

> "What is *Real?* . . . Does it mean having things that buzz inside
> you and a stick-out handle?" "Real isn't how you are made," said
> the Skin Horse. "It's a thing that happens to you. When a child
> loves you for a long, long time, not just to play with, but REALLY
> loves you, then you become Real."
>
> "Does it hurt?" asked the Rabbit.
>
> "Sometimes," said the Skin Horse, for he was always truthful.
> "When you are real you don't mind being hurt."

"Does it happen all at once, like being wound up," he asked, "or bit by bit?"

"It doesn't happen all at once," said the Skin Horse. "You become. It takes a long time. That's why it doesn't often happen to people who break easily, or have sharp edges, or who have to be carefully kept. Generally, by the time you are Real, most of your hair has been loved off, and your eyes drop out and you get loose in the joints and very shabby. But these things don't matter at all, because once you are Real you can't be ugly, except to people who don't understand."

"I suppose *you* are Real?" said the Rabbit. . . .

"The Boy's uncle made me Real," he said. "That was a great many years ago; but once you are Real you can't become unreal again. It lasts for always."[9]

That is how God became real: when he came in Jesus of Nazareth, flesh of our vulnerable flesh, giving himself to us in the risk of human loving. And that is how we become real: as we have first been loved by God in Christ and as we now engage in the service of love. Such love is not only acting but also being acted upon; so it is inevitably suffering love, as all true love is.

But therein is real life and it is the gospel's answer to the breaking of hearts. In the breaking of hearts, Christ enters in to comfort and to call. Oscar Wilde is reported to have said on his deathbed: "How else but through a broken heart / May Lord Christ enter in?"[10] Only in the breaking of hearts do we receive and give the balm of grace. All because in the breaking of the one great heart of Christ we and all the world have entered into the vast common room of God's eternal love. There our hearts are mended and renewed.

Notes

1. Wayne Oates, *The Presence of God in Pastoral Counseling* (Waco: Word Books, 1986), Chapter 6.

2. Moule, p. 5.

3. My teacher Daniel Day Williams used this definition often. See his book *The Spirit and Forms of Love* (New York: Harper & Row, 1968).

4. *King Lear,* III, 4, 28.

5. E. Glenn Hinson, *Identity and Adaptability: The Role of Selected Ecclesiastical and Theological Forms in the Early Christian Mission Until A.D. 451* (Oxford Dissertation, 1973), pp. 458-514. See also his book, *The Evangelization of the Roman Empire: Identity and Adaptability* (Macon, Ga.: Mercer University Press, 1981).

6. Concerning the last theological movement I would recommend: Richard Shaull, *Heralds of a New Reformation: The Poor of South and North America* (Maryknoll, New York: Orbis Books, 1984).

Robert McAfee Brown, *Theology in a New Key* (Philadelphia: The Westminster Press, 1978).

Letty Russell, *Human Liberation in a Feminist Perspective—A Theology* (Philadelphia: Westminster Press, 1974).

Gustavo Gutierrez, *A Theology of Liberation* (Maryknoll, New York: Orbis, 1972).

James Cone, *God of the Oppressed* (New York: The Seabury Press, 1975).

7. William Sloan Coffin, *The Courage to Love* (San Francisco: Harper & Row, 1984), p. 86.

8. John Donne, *Devotions Upon Emergent Occasions* (Oxford: Oxford University Press, 1987), p. 87.

9. Margery Williams, *The Velveteen Rabbit* (New York: Doubleday & Co., n.d.) pp. 16-20.

10. Oscar Wilde, "The Ballad of Reading Gaol," st. 14, *Bartlett's Familiar Quotations* (Boston: Little Brown and Co., 1980), p. 676.

3

Paul and His Troubles,
or "All My Trials, Lord"

(1:8 to 2:13; 7:5-16)

Paul was no university professor dropping pipe ash on his cor-
duroy jacket as he sat in his tenured chair in some quaint ivy-
covered office building. He was a traveling preacher/
organizer/evangelist/teacher called by blinding light and resurrection voice to trample at the risk of life and sanity across the
Mediterranean world with a gospel so good it had made him its
slave. He was a brilliant and flawed human being, and his letters
arose out of the tender and tough associations with beginning
churches and new Christians in the hostile world of competing
religions, but also a hungry world longing for the gospel.

His letters, therefore, are cut from the same cloth as our own
most human lives; acquainted with both the sublime and the ridic-
ulous, riddled with conflict, envy, and mistrust, and as full of
danger and darkness as of beauty and light. In these letters we
catch glimpse of family argument, disruption of friendship, quar-
relsome church business meetings, and the ordinary quotient of
human cruelty, sickness, and sin. (As someone said, "total de-
pravity" is a good-enough doctrine if we could only live up to it!)
But out of this most human context we get a glimpse of eternal
truth so wonderful it is Scripture for us, an eternal truth shining
through our cracked earthen pots.

The gospel was spread in the midst of ordinary and extraordinary trials and tribulations. To some of these we now turn.

Deliverance from Death and Despair
1:8-11

Paul informs the Corinthians of his most recent deliverance by
the hand of God. We cannot know for sure which calamity Paul is

referring to here, but it is probably located somewhere in his list of afflictions in chapter 11 (vv. 12-27). My own best guess is that Paul is referring to an experience of imprisonment which included physical beatings and the sentencing of death by execution. But what Paul faces is more than the prospect of death administered by hostile outside forces. He also wrestles with the inner darkness of despair. The language vividly portrays this double darkness: FOR WE WERE SO UTTERLY, UNBEARABLY CRUSHED ["crushed far beyond what I could stand" translates Moffatt] THAT WE DESPAIRED OF LIFE ITSELF. WHY, WE FELT THAT WE HAD RECEIVED THE SENTENCE OF DEATH (1:8-9).

Here was an awesome conjunction of afflictions, physical, emotional, spiritual. He is probably physically very weak: there is a death sentence hanging over his head. Add to all this a despair over the absurdity of God's messenger of good news about to be done in. As Victor Frankl discovered from his concentration camp experience, we can endure untold suffering as long as we can find meaning in our affliction.[1] Meaning itself is the essential survival tool, but it appears that Paul was close to losing meaning too.

But deliverance came! And as it came Paul discovered the meaning of this experience of distress and despair: BUT THAT WAS TO MAKE US RELY NOT ON OURSELVES BUT ON GOD WHO RAISES THE DEAD (v. 10). In his human weakness Paul suffered despair, but the deliverance had taught him (again and again we learn this lesson) to rely not on himself but on God who raises the dead. So Paul expresses gratitude for this deliverance and for the rebirth of hope in the God who continues to deliver.

It is the crucified Messiah who has entered Paul's darkness with him. And into all our darkness, too. In Peter Kreeft's words:

He came. He entered space and time and suffering. He came, like a lover. . . . He sits beside us in the lowest places of our lives, like water. Are we broken? He is broken with us. Are we rejected? . . . He was "despised and rejected of me." . . . Do we weep? . . . He was "a man of sorrow and acquainted with grief." . . . Does he descend into all our hells? Yes. In the unforgettable line of Corrie ten Boom from the depths of Nazi death camp, "No matter how deep our darkness, he is deeper still."[2]

Howard Thurman's book *The Luminous Darkness* takes its title from the experience of a deep-sea diver who describes his descent. First there is the belt of fishes, a wide band of light reflecting the surface of the sea. then the diver moves into a depth of water that cannot be penetrated by the light above the surface. It is dark and foreboding. The diver is apt to feel panic; but as he drops deeper into the abyss, "slowly his eyes begin to pick up the luminous quality of the darkness," and his fear is relaxed.[3] Paul has gone deep enough to experience the luminous darkness of God's sea.

Trouble in the Church ### 1:12 to 2:13; 7:5-16

This letter grows out of a long-term relationship with Corinth, a relationship intense and stormy. There is not the easy affection noticeable in Paul's correspondence to the Philippians, but the bonding is strong. They need one another. Conflict has tested the relationship over and over again.

In his first visit to Corinth, Paul had founded the church. First Corinthians was written after that founding visit and attempted to settle some problems which had cropped up—with mixed success. But 1 Corinthians was not really first. In 1 Corinthians 5:9, Paul mentions a previous letter he had written them, and 1 Corinthians, in part, deals with misunderstandings concerning that previous letter.

Then there was another visit by Paul to Corinth. In that visit, there was a painful and public confrontation by a "brother" in the church (2:1-11). Paul left shaken. In the aftermath he wrote another letter (the third in our count), now lost, a painful and tearful one: FOR I WROTE YOU OUT OF MUCH AFFLICTION AND ANGUISH OF HEART AND WITH MANY TEARS (2:4).

Paul wrote this letter and canceled a promised visit. He did this, in his mind, to spare them the pain of another visit (v. 1). Evidently the offending brother was still there, the problem unresolved, and Paul felt a personal visit at that time would solve nothing. So for now the letter would have to do, a letter confronting the brother, speaking to the problem, and asking the church's help in dealing with it.

Some of the church accused Paul of being fickle and unreliable in not making the scheduled visit. WAS I VACILLATING? Paul asks rhetorically (1:17). And Paul is terribly anxious as to how the church will respond to the letter. We do not know the exact nature of the conflict, but it appears to be bound up in the larger issues of the letter. The brother was probably challenging Paul's apostolic authority openly and with untrue charges. This represented a crisis for Paul—could he still have apostolic leadership among them—and for the church—who is telling the truth, what is the real gospel, who are the real apostles? And if the brother is wrong, how are they to discipline him and preserve the integrity of the community?

Paul not only feels attacked by the adversary but also feels underdefended by the church at the time of the attack (7:5-16). What pastor has not felt abandoned by the silent majority of the church when an individual or minority faction has attacked him? Paul limped away from the confrontation feeling wounded by the attacker and grieved by the lack of defense given him by the church.

So, Paul's letter is tearfully written and fearfully too—how would the congregation respond? What would they do about the brother? How human Paul is as he describes his high anxiety while he awaits their response! He is *miserable*—just as we all are when we write a loved one a confrontational letter and wait for a response. Every day seems an eternity as we anxiously await the mailman or a phone call.

Paul has sent the letter by Titus and now fitfully waits a response. In fact, he goes to Troas to preach, expecting Titus to meet him there with the news, but when Titus does not appear, Paul writes, MY MIND COULD NOT REST (2:13) and he packs his bags and goes to Macedonia, eyes hungry to see Titus.

Second Corinthians glows with thanksgiving for the good news Titus *finally* brought (and now we move to 7:5 *ff.*). The people responded well. They heard Paul's pain, took defense of him, and disciplined the offending brother. They did not get angry in response to Paul's confrontation. Whew! You could have heard Paul's sigh of relief all across Macedonia.

This moves us to consideration of two pastoral issues: intimacy and distance of the pastor/church relationship, and what happens when the people say no?

Intimacy and Distance

What we see in Paul is the necessary combination of intimacy and distance every pastor/church relationship needs—and *every* important relationship needs. Here is another paradoxical image of ministry, as Fred Craddock identifies it in Paul and names it for us: "intimate distance."[4] Paul is close enough to be deeply hurt by the conflict, yet he is distant enough to be free to confront the church. You can be so close you cannot confront; you can be so aloof that confrontation is easy, painless, and frequent (for the confronter, that is). Paul exercises the passionate and painful combination of intimacy and distance. Intimacy says with Paul OUR MOUTH IS OPEN TO YOU, CORINTHIANS; OUR HEART IS WIDE (6:11). Intimacy risks saying: IN RETURN—I SPEAK AS TO CHILDREN—WIDEN YOUR HEARTS ALSO (v. 13).

The good pastor (and parent and spouse and friend) discovers the intimacy in distance and distance in intimacy that every relationship needs. As pastor, the minister needs to be the person who conveys the parental closeness of God and friendship of Jesus. But as prophet, the minister reminds the people that God is Holy Other, always calling them to be holy in their humanness. In some ways, the pastor is like a spouse to the church; the covenant is that intimate and mutually responsible. But in fact the church is the bride of Christ, not the bride of the pastor, and the pastor at times needs to drop back a bit, take some distance, so that the church recognizes its sacred responsibility to Christ, an allegiance superseding that with the pastor. The congregation does not belong to the pastor, but to Christ.

This is not an incidental issue to the letter, for super-apostles would LORD IT OVER the congregation taking the authority belonging only to Christ. Paul would instead be a SERVANT sometimes bearing Christ's authority but always pointing beyond himself to Christ. The church's one foundation is not Paul, but Christ.

Intimate distance—neither professional aloofness, nor unhealthy closeness is what Paul exhibited. It is at times an agonizing combination; it would be easier to have one or the other. But such is the path of all true (suffering) love. What parent does not need both intimacy and distance with a child? A parent's love can be so close as to destroy both parent and child. What marriage, what important friendship, does not need both?

Second Corinthians is a marvelous window open to this pastor/church relationship. And we learn. It would have been easy for Paul to be so disappointed with the Corinthians as to write them off. It would have been easy for Paul to have stayed so close that he refused to confront. It would have been easy to assume the posture of Lord and lay on them an ultimatum. But Paul hangs in there with them, he confronts within a relationship of covenant love, as their servant not their lord, and with a love the Old Testament calls *hesed,* the steadfast covenant love of God, the patient, persistent, stubborn, never-giving-up-no-matter-what love of God, but a love willing to take the human risk of losing the relationship in order that the relationship be healthy and strong. It was a risk Paul was willing to take because he knew the ultimate relationship the church needed was not with him, but with Jesus Christ.

When the People Say No

To be sure, at least some of the people were saying no to Paul. If the SUPER-APOSTLES were gaining no foothold and no followers in the congregation, Paul would have felt no threat. What happens when the people say no?

Ministry means suffering, the suffering of vulnerable human love, the suffering of so many unanswered prayers, uncertain results, and unbidden noes. To watch as people go on self-destructive binges, to see marriages end and children go astray, to hear people say no to you, no to God (the two not necessarily the same), no to the church, and no to life and joy is a *sorrow.*

James Dittes says that ministry is "grief work."[5] What he means is the sorrow of watching death at work. And it involves the noes people say to us and to the gospel. We are called to give ourselves away in prodigal love to a people who cannot sustain the vision God calls us to embody together. None of us (including, if we are honest, us professional ministers) can live up to it, so we every day grieve our own limits and our people's incapacities, stubbornesses, and failures.

So we must learn to do *good* grief work, that is, working through our disappointments and discouragements, yes, our griefs in ways that let us still minister compassionately and creatively and help God's people go forward into the life His kingdom promises us.

People's noes cause us grief, says Dittes, but we must learn to take them seriously and listen to them so that we can hear the deeper message and deeper pain underneath. For noes are often inarticulate groans of the Spirit arising out of pain. As Paul wrote: "Likewise the Spirit helps us in our weakness; for we do not know how to pray as we ought, but the Spirit himself intercedes for us with sighs too deep for words" (Rom. 8:26). Compassionate ministers listen for the sighs and groans of the noes. As such we listen as partners rather than adversaries. When noes come from anger, instead of quickly lashing back we must patiently search for the pain behind the anger. Noes will bruise our hearts, but if we can keep our bruised egos out of the way we can listen with compassion.

The compassionate ministers are able to listen because they recognize that this grief and our grief and all grief is part of the common weeping. There should be no grief completely foreign to the minister.

Jesus forewarned Peter by the seaside as he called him to be a shepherd of his flock:

> Truly, truly, I say to you, when you were young, you girded yourself and walked where you would; but when you are old, you will stretch out your hands, and another will gird you and carry you where you do not wish to go (John 21:18).

When we ministers are young, we think we will always be able to do everything we want to do, lead where we want to lead, and go where we want to go. We will not minister long before we will hear noes and be carried where we do not want to go. People's noes and our powerlessness are not, however, denials of our ministry. They can be our greatest teachers. We can respond to people's noes as *ruler*—and respond with anger and control—or as *victim*—and respond as helpless martyr. And if we do, true ministry will end. But if we respond as *learner,* we and our people will go to finer ministry together.

Notes

1. Victor Frankl, *Man's Search for Meaning* (New York: Washington Square Press, 1963).

2. Peter Kreeft, *Making Sense Out of Suffering* (Ann Arbor: Servant Books, 1986), pp. 133-134.

3. Howard Thurman, *The Luminous Darkness* (New York: Harper & Row, 1965), p. VII.

4. Fred Craddock, *Philippians* in Interpretation Commentary (Atlanta: John Knox Press, 1985), p. 6.

5. James Dittes, *When the People Say No* (New York: Harper & Row Publishers, 1979).

4
God's Encircling Yes

(1:15-20)

Here is resurrection dawn, the light of God's encircling yes. Even the deepest darkness is luminous with God's light. Paul began this paragraph defending himself against the charges of unreliability over his not coming on a promised visit to Corinth. WAS I VACILLATING? he asked (v. 17). But now he launches into a lyrical burst of song: FOR THE SON OF GOD, JESUS CHRIST, WHOM WE PREACHED AMONG YOU, . . . WAS NOT YES AND NO; BUT IN HIM IT IS ALWAYS YES. FOR ALL THE PROMISES OF GOD FIND THEIR YES IN HIM (vv. 19-20).

In Jesus Christ God has spoken his yes, the final yes, the everlasting yes, the *encircling yes*.

I

Sometimes in creation we sense God's yes. So Gerard Manly Hopkins saw,

> Glory be to God for dappled things.

And Edna St. Vincent Millay,

> O world, I cannot hold thee close enough!

Or e. e. cummings,

> i thank you God for this most amazing
> day: for the leaping greenly spirits of trees
> and a blue true dream of sky; and for everything
> which is natural which is infinite which is yes.[1]

A proper theology of creation senses God's yes in creation. Karl Barth, perhaps one of this century's greatest theologians, called

Mozart "a theologian of creation." In "an open letter" of thanks
to Mozart he wrote:

> What I thank you for is simply this, that whenever I hear you I find
> myself set in the threshold of a good and orderly world, both in
> rain and sunshine and by day and night.[2]

Barth said that Mozart displayed in his music a knowledge of creation "in its total goodness" that few, if any, of the church's theologians have known or expressed. Mozart heard "the harmony of
creation to which the shadow belongs, but in which the shadow is
not darkness, deficiency is not defeat, sadness cannot become despair." There is darkness all right, in creation and in our human
ways, but in Mozart's music "the light shines all the more brightly
because it breaks forth from the shadow." Mozart, said Barth,
"heard all creation enveloped by this light."[3] God's encircling yes.

But creation alone cannot reveal God's yes. Yes is what Paul
sees in Christ as he bursts into the song: FOR THE SON OF
GOD, JESUS CHRIST, WHOM WE PREACHED . . . IS NOT
YES AND NO; BUT IN HIM IT IS ALWAYS YES.

Creation is not enough to show us God's shining face. Jesus
Christ has preeminently made him known, and in so doing shines
forth God's yes. God sent him into the world "not to condemn the
world, but that the world might be saved through him" (John
3:17). He came among us, God's yes enfleshed. He was
". . . surprise of Mercy, outgoing Gladness, Rescue, Healing and
Life."[4] Yes. He befriended the lonely, those lonely for friends, for
love, for God. He healed the sick and healed sinners. Yes was
what he spoke and lived.

And *died*. He gave his life as a ransom. From that cross we
heard the astonishing, "Forgive them." How much more could
God have demonstrated his love than this, "that while we were
[still being] sinners Christ died for us" (Rom. 5:8).

And *rose*. The resurrection is the dawn of yes shedding a softer,
kinder light on Creation, a dawn announcing the final dawn. It is
evidence of God's power, the triumph of life over death, of right
over wrong and of light over all the darkness we and all the powers
of earth can muster. It is also the evidence of God's unconquerable

love, a love that even in the face of our killing his Son, will not let us go, a love made eloquent in suffering which shall finally be triumphant love. God's encircling yes.

II

The gospel of God's yes, however, is surprisingly hard to hear. It fights with most our experiences and too much of our theology. Our world is so full of mixed messages. Not the clear, simple *yes,* but rather *yes and no; yes, but; yes, if. . . .*

Our family of origin provides the deepest pool of messages, messages which continue to color our emotions all our lives. There is the conditional *yes, if.* If we are good, we expect to hear yes; if we are bad, we expect to hear no. If we succeed, we get yes; if we fail, we get no. No wonder God's unconditional yes is so hard to hear. We project onto God all the mixed messages that come from our past and present.

Some of us grow up never hearing yes, only a succession of scolding, critical noes. We know we will never measure up. Never can we hope to see our parents' faces break into delight in us. God becomes condemning, critical Judge.

Even worse is the false yes and no some parents deliver. We cannot trust the yes to be yes and the no to be no. In his work *Obsessive Children,* psychiatrist Paul L. Adams documents the damage done by a mother who gives mixed messages, who smiles while destroying others with her tongue, "covering brutality with sweet undoing talk,"[5] who says yes with her mask of a face but no with her emotions and actions. Her child grows up continually uncertain, willing to sacrifice everything, even sense of true self, in order to please the parent and escape her wrath. *Yes, but.*

Or, think of the children of alcoholics who can never predict when the yes or no will come, for alcoholic addiction has produced in the parent erratic, frightfully unpredictable patterns of affection and abuse. It is *yes and no,* but we never know when or why and we internalize the blame, taking responsibility for the parent's behavior.

The family is the deepest, most powerful source of these messages, but society gives them to us as well through sex roles and class distinctions, through school and neighborhoods, in church and synagogue which sometimes challenge the surrounding cultural values but too often reflect them.

But these are gods carved out of human experience. Jesus Christ has shown us the true face of God, and it shines with yes. Not *yes and no,* but *yes, but,* not *yes, if.* Yes!

God is not a neurotic parent manipulating us with cruel or capricious patterns of yes and no and turning us into his fearful and insecure children. He's *Abba* Father who loves us with an unconditional, encircling yes. He has spoken his yes, acted his yes, lived and died his yes in Jesus Christ. And in this Christ we hear and experience this yes.

To be sure there are noes that need to be spoken and heard in the nurturing and training of the children of God. But these *noes* are not the last word, the last word is always *yes.* The no is always spoken within the deeper yes.

Paul is accused of breaking his promise. Paul answers that he is reliable, but more than that, that God is reliable, for ALL GOD'S PROMISES FIND THEIR YES IN JESUS CHRIST.

That is the gospel we preach. God is for us, not against us. In spite of everything, yes! Through all the events of Jesus' life, death, and resurrection and in fervent hope of his final triumphant return, we hear yes!

III

That is God's great act. What is our response? God has said yes. We say amen. God has acted his yes; we now act our amen.

Amen. It means so be it. Let it be. Amen is the yes we utter back to God. It is always a thankful yes. That is our wondrous calling: to utter amen, to sing it, and live it.

We do so with our lips in worship's praise. Worship is the continuous exclamation amen to the mighty works, grace, and blessing of God. We do so with our lives as we engage in the service of love and speaking God's yes to the world.

Of course, we do not do it on our own. THROUGH HIM [Christ], WE UTTER OUR AMEN TO THE GLORY OF GOD (1:20).

Jesus Christ was not only God's *yes* to us; he is also our *amen* back to God. In his perfect obedience and even more perfect love, he was and is our amen. And as he lives in us who follow him, we find ourselves saying—always with our best selves—amen. In our creeds and confessions, we say amen with our minds. In our thankful hymns and prayers, we say amen with our hearts. In our glad obedience, the service of love, we say amen with our bodies.

Yes, God's gracious act. *Amen,* our joyful calling in the answering of our lives.

Notes

1. e. e. cummings, *100 Selected Poems* (New York: Grove Press, Inc., 1959), p. 114.

2. Karl Barth, *Final Testimonies,* ed. Eberhard Busch (Grand Rapids, Mich.: Wm. B. Eerdmans, 1977), p. 19.

3. Karl Barth, *Church Dogmatics* (Edinburgh: T&T Clark, 1961), III/3:297-299.

4. George Buttrick, *Prayer* (New York: Abingdon Press, 1942), p. 83.

5. Paul L. Adams, *Obsessive Children* (New York: Penguin Books, 1973), p. 71.

5
The Humiliating Triumph:
A Hymn

(2:14-16)

In these three verses, Paul sets forth what Collange calls the major theme of the letter. It is in the form of "a little hymn,"[1] a hymn of humiliation and triumph. THANKS TO GOD. It images a kind of apostle quite different from that of the super-apostles. Paul sings thanks to God who IN CHRIST ALWAYS LEADS US IN TRIUMPH. But Christ's apostles do not play the part of the victors leading the triumphal procession through the city streets. Rather, they are the victims who trail the conquerer bound as slaves. The Christians are put on display as prisoners in a triumphal procession. As Moffatt translates the phrase, HE MAKES MY LIFE A CONSTANT PAGEANT OF TRIUMPH (v. 14).

The humiliating triumph. Moffatt's translation vividly captures the enigmatic character of the image—which fits with the paradoxical images of ministry all through the letter. We are led in triumph, but we are the humiliated ones who triumph in their humiliation. We are those who serve in weakness. This image of apostleship is very close to the one Paul presents in 1 Corinthians.

> For I think that God has exhibited us apostles as last of all, like men sentenced to death; because we have become a spectacle to the world, to angels and to men. We are fools for Christ's sake, but you are wise in Christ. We are weak, but you are strong. You are held in honor, but we are in disrepute (4:9-10).

"I thank you God that you drag us through the streets humiliated victims of your great triumph!" Is this what Paul was saying, singing? I think so. And it is not so far from that extraordinary prayer from Jesus' lips when he realized what was happening to his own mission:

62

I thank thee, Father, Lord of heaven and earth, that thou has hidden these things from the wise and understanding and revealed them to babes; yea, Father, for such was thy gracious will (Matt. 11:25-26).

We may look weak, says Paul, but that's all to the glory of God. It's all part of the victory procession of the kingdom of God.

So Paul begins with an image for the eyes, the sight of Christ leading a triumphal procession of apostle-slaves. Now he adds smell. Thanks to God who THROUGH US SPREADS THE FRAGRANCE OF THE KNOWLEDGE OF HIM EVERY-WHERE. The ancient military procession often burned incense as part of the pomp and circumstance.

I love the image of knowledge of God as sweet aroma. Knowledge of God is inexhaustible pleasure, and it is a knowledge located precisely in Jesus the Christ (and therefore is not just any smell but a particular aroma). And it is a knowledge that spreads through the air as unstoppable as any fragrance.

WE ARE THE AROMA OF CHRIST TO GOD. As the fragrance of Christ we spread the sweet smell of Christ's love throughout the world. Our lives are first, however, offered to God as living sacrifices and as such also become a sweet aroma to God. Sacrifice is not a word which the world likes very much. It sounds like, smells like death to the world, but in fact it is the smell of life, real life, the life of love that takes a servant's form.

Annie Dillard watched a moth fly into a candle flame and catch fire, its body becoming a wick bearing the candle flame. It became for her a metaphor of the Christian life and the artist's life:

> There is no such thing as an artist: there is only the world lit or unlit as the light allows. When the candle is burning, who looks at the wick? When the candle is out, who needs it? But the world without light is wasteland and chaos, and a life without sacrifice is abomination.[2]

We are like the moth flying to the flame of God's holy love. Our very bodies have become wicks lighting the world with Christ's light and sending forth the sweet smell of the knowledge of God.

To the world sacrifice is itself an abomination. Life is in self-mastery, self-realization, self-fulfillment. To the followers of Christ, however, life without sacrifice is abomination, for we believe that life is in self-giving, in making ourselves self-forgetful (and living) sacrifices of love. We follow the one who said: "For whoever would save his life will lose it; and whoever loses his life for my sake and the gospel's will save it" (Mark 8:35). Here is a riddle understood only by those who are being saved, that is, those who are following him who said these words.

To the world it sounds foolish, but it is the true wisdom. To the world such smell of sacrifice smells like death, but it is in fact the sweet perfume of life, real life, eternal life. FOR WE ARE THE AROMA OF CHRIST TO GOD AMONG THOSE WHO ARE BEING SAVED AND AMONG THOSE WHO ARE PERISHING, TO ONE A FRAGRANCE FROM DEATH TO DEATH, TO THE OTHER A FRAGRANCE FROM LIFE TO LIFE (v. 15).

An analogy from life. Hospitals have a strongly identifiable smell. Some people cannot stand the smell. It smells to them of pain and death. But to others it smells of clean sheets and scrubbed floors and walls and of the holy, almost monkish rigors of medical education and practice. To one it smells of sickness and death, to another life and hope of healing. So we, the aroma of Christ, will smell like death to some and like life to others.

These short verses, a short hymn of humiliation and triumph, set the major tone of the book: what looks like a humiliating march of defeat is in fact a triumphal procession, and what smells like death to some is in fact the sweet aroma of the knowledge of God and the love of Christ. It is a fragrance which is spilling into the air, unstoppable, ever sweetening the air we breathe with the scent of love.

Notes

1. So says Windisch cited in Furnish, p. 185.
2. Annie Dillard, *Holy the Firm* (New York: Harper & Row, 1977) pp. 71-72.

6
A Letter of Christ: First Round of Defense

(2:17 to 3:6)

Paul begins his explicit defense of his apostleship with these verses. Keep in mind here as everywhere in the letter that as he defends his apostleship he also defines the nature of true apostolic ministry for the whole church. It is *our* ministry he defends. FOR WE ARE NOT, LIKE SO MANY, PEDDLERS OF GOD'S WORD; BUT AS MEN OF SINCERITY, AS COMMISSIONED BY GOD (2:17). Others peddle God's word like wine merchants in the street, watering it down for higher profit. But not Paul; he speaks only out of divine calling with SINCERITY. Karl Barth wrote of this verse:

> The word of God is not for sale; and therefore it has no need of shrewd salesmen. . . . It does not care to be sold at any price. It only desires to be its own genuine self, without being compelled to suffer alterations and modifications. . . . Until then, it can afford to lie on its shelf and wait as if it were poor merchandise.[1]

WHO IS SUFFICIENT FOR THESE THINGS? (v. 17). No one. Only they who depend on God and God alone for their sufficiency are the ministers. Paul is having to defend himself, and he hates it. He knows the folly of it, so he is "like a motorist who drives with his brakes on."[2] But defend himself he must, for the truth of the gospel is at stake. Super-apostles have come to town waving their fancy letters of recommendation. "Where is *your* letter?" they challenge Paul.

You, my church at Corinth, ARE OUR LETTER OF RECOMMENDATION, Paul answers. It is not a letter written on paper, but a letter WRITTEN ON YOUR HEARTS, TO BE KNOWN

AND READ BY ALL MEN (3:2). If Paul needs a letter of recommendation, the only one that counts is the letter written by the life of the congregation at Corinth, or the letter which is the life of the congregation.

Again, moving from personal defense to definition of the church, Paul says, YOU ARE A LETTER FROM CHRIST (v. 3). What an intriguing image of the church—a letter from Christ. And if we are a communication from Christ to the world, we first and last are a love letter.

Some letters that churches send the world are far from love letters. Some are Dear John letters: "Too bad, world, you messed up." Some are chain letters promising more than Jesus ever promised: "Just send your contribution and God will bless you." Some letters are exclusive engraved invitations: "RSVP, White Tie." Other letters are eviction notices, rejection slips, or report cards: they carry condemnation; they say no.

But as the church, we are a love letter from Christ. We say in Christ, "Come, . . . who labor and are heavy laden, and I will give you rest" (Matt. 11:28). We say, "[Your sins are forgiven,] go and sin no more" (John 8:11, KJV). We say, "[Come,] enter thou into the joy of thy Lord" (Matt. 25:21,23, KJV).

We the church are a letter from Christ: we are by miracle of grace and not in our own power the ongoing incarnation of Christ. But this letter, since it is an incarnational message, is written NOT WITH INK BUT WITH THE SPIRIT OF GOD. It is written NOT ON TABLETS OF STONE BUT ON TABLETS OF HUMAN HEARTS (3:3).

We are MINISTERS OF A NEW COVENANT who serve not IN A WRITTEN CODE BUT IN THE SPIRIT (v. 6). Paul argues his gospel against a version of the gospel being foisted upon the people, a version which is no gospel at all. The opponents are evidently preaching the old Mosaic covenant, TABLETS OF STONE. Moses is the true hero; his law is the centerpiece. Jesus is merely one like Moses.

In contrast, Paul preached the new covenant of grace, the law of love, Christ's love. And it is a possibility for us because the Spirit of the Lord renews our hearts. True religion is not a straitjacket of laws trying to tame the outer self, but is the "renewal of heart." So easily does the living law of God become an icy legalism and literal truth become a proud prison of literalism. But where is there the Spirit of the living God? Nowhere. True faith comes by the Spirit, and there is life, FOR THE WRITTEN CODE KILLS BUT THE SPIRIT GIVES LIFE (v. 6).

This is not an incidental issue for Paul. Stephen had preached Christ as the New Torah replacing, fulfilling the OLD, and Paul had assisted in his being stoned to death. Then, miracle of grace, the living Christ appeared to Paul and Paul discovered that it is in the living Spirit of the Lord, not in the dead letters of the OLD COVENANT that we find our life.

Hope is not in the policing of the self—the way of the law—but is in what Collange calls *la renovation des coerus, the renewal (or renovation!) of hearts,* "the one total and radical renovation of the human person"[3] which is the way of the Spirit.

Notes

1. Karl Barth and Edward Thurneysen, *Come Holy Spirit* (Grand Rapids, Mich.: W. B. Eerdmans, 1978), p. 219.

2. Beasley-Murray, p. 6.

3. Collange, p. 66, translation mine.

7

Transfiguration:
Divine Men or the People of God
Being Transformed

(3:7-18)

At the beach I watched a gull swoop and soar in the late afternoon. The sun was behind the house on whose back porch I sat so I couldn't see it except for the moments when this gull, which was dark on top and white underneath, would sweep through the air, then, for a glorious moment, turn her whiteness to the sun and reflect the most blinding white-gold light. There she was just for a moment, shining like the sun. She wasn't just white anymore, but the sun's very gleaming gold-white blinding light. Was that what the children of Israel saw on Moses' face as he descended Mount Sinai or what the disciples saw on Jesus' face on the mount of transfiguration? Or what Paul himself saw on the road to Damascus? A human face now shining like the sun? Shining with the glory of God?

Paul plays with such imagery as he addresses the transformation of the Christian in the Spirit of the Lord. There is a kind of transfiguration at work in the life of the Christian, but it is a peculiar kind of transfiguration.

The gospel of Jesus Christ is a gospel of transformation. Isn't that our deepest longing? The ancient philosopher Seneca said, "I would I were not so much bettered as transformed." We grow tired of piddling self-improvement courses. We despair of another round of New Year's resolutions. We want transformation. We want to shine like the sun.

Paul talks of transformation in these verses as the SPLENDOR of shining with the glory of God. But he uses the image as part of a polemic against the super-apostles and their brand of transformation. It is impossible to understand these verses apart from this controversy. Scholars like Georgi and Collange have helped us reconstruct the picture of these opponents.[1] They saw themselves as "divine-men" in a divine continuum from Moses to Jesus to themselves. Moses' face shone with the glory of God at Sinai, Jesus' face shone at the mount of transfiguration, and now the super-apostles could make their faces shine through ecstatic experiences. They followed Moses' law perfectly and their faces shone like the face of Moses as he returned from Sinai. Evidently Exodus 34:29-35 was a key passage for these opponents, and so Paul reinterprets that passage, in his mind the right way.

In verses 7-11 Paul summarizes the Old Testament story of the giving of the law and Moses coming down from Sinai, his face shining with God's glory. But Paul quickly adds that this glory of the Old Covenant is passing away. The greater glory of the New Covenant is found in Jesus Christ, and it is not fading away. Again, Paul contrasts the fading glory of the Law with the greater splendor of the Spirit of the Living God.

In verse 13 Paul moves beyond the Old Testament narrative to reinterpret the meaning of the VEIL Moses put over his face. Paul says it was to cover up the fading glory. This is a new preachment from Paul. Neither the Old Testament nor rabbinic tradition has anything like it. Was Paul testifying to the futility of salvation by works? The one who lives by the Law is always anxious about the fading glory. Your face may shine at the first receiving of the Law but you can never perfectly keep it, so anxiety fills your heart and you hide your face in shame to keep the truth from being too obvious: I can't keep the Law.

Not only does the VEIL hide our shame, it also keeps us from understanding of the Old Covenant. But when we turn to the Lord and let his SPIRIT enter us, THE VEIL IS REMOVED and we experience FREEDOM. We not only shine, we fly!

Now Paul moves more deeply to the contrast between the transformation offered by the super-apostles and that experienced by the apostolic church. The super-apostles try to make themselves shine through perfect obedience or by ecstatic experience.

Paul says, in contrast, that we are being changed by the Spirit of the Living God. Does this passage not lift our hearts and hopes?

AND WE ALL, WITH UNVEILED FACE, BEHOLDING THE
GLORY OF THE LORD, ARE BEING CHANGED INTO HIS
LIKENESS FROM ONE DEGREE OF GLORY TO ANOTHER
(3:18). The image is of gazing into a mirror and seeing the glory
of God, or of reflecting that glory as a mirror.

Note these important qualifiers. WE ALL: transformation is
not for an elite corp of super-apostles, but for the whole people of
God. ARE BEING CHANGED: transformation is not instanta-
neous. It is FROM ONE DEGREE to another. We are not perfect.
We are being changed, being· redeemed. We are the "assuredly
broken yet being-saved" community of God. And it comes by BE-
HOLDING THE GLORY OF THE LORD.

We become what we behold. It is true enough on a purely human level. We take on the characteristics (for better and for
worse) of those we look upon. That's why husbands and wives
often begin to look alike after having lived together a long time.
Unconsciously we mimic the mannerisms and expressions of the
other.

Nathaniel Hawthorne tells in a short story called "The Great
Stone Face" of a village towered over by a huge stone cliff. On the
face of the cliff nature had carved what appeared to be a great
stone face, god-like, noble in features, grand and sweet in expression, casting over the whole village the sense of well-being.

The story tells of Ernest, who from a young age, was fascinated
by the Great Stone Face. Untold hours he spent studying that face.
He often heard the old legend told by villagers: one day a child
would be born whose likeness would perfectly match that face.
Every time a person would visit the town, Ernest and all the villagers would look expectantly to see if the faces matched. But, no.

From boyhood through adolescence, manhood and older adult-
hood, Ernest spent all his free hours gazing at the face.

Then one day as he was talking to some of the villagers, they
looked at the Great Stone Face and then at Ernest and exclaimed:

"Behold! Behold! Ernest himself is the likeness of the Great
Stone Face."[2]

Such is the mystery of the church as she beholds the Christ.
Little by little, degree by degree, as we gaze upon him, we are
being changed into his likeness.

When we look at Christ and learn of Christ, we are changed—
we begin to be like Christ, to follow him and become obedient as
he was obedient, to love with his love.

Is that too much to expect? Is Paul just an idealist? Of course,
we do not do this on our own. It is not our work. This human flesh
cannot muster up enough to be like Christ. It, like everything else
in the Christian life, is a gift. It is grace. So Paul adds, FOR THIS
COMES FROM THE LORD WHO IS THE SPIRIT.

Who establishes us to speak our amen? Only Christ.

Who is sufficient to be the aroma of Christ? No one except
through Christ.

What is our competence to be the letter of Christ? Only the
Spirit of Christ.

Who changes us from one degree of glory to another into the
likeness of Christ? It is the Lord.

The transformation is not instant obedience to the law of God,
nor is it the spectacular and temporary experience of ecstacy. It is
the continual transformation of the heart by the patient Spirit of
God as we, degree by degree, are being changed into Christ's likeness. And this likeness has less to do with a hero's handsome face
than with the face of a suffering servant ennobled with the pain of
life. It has less to do with moral perfection and more to do with the
compassionate heart. It has less to do with brilliant insights and
more to do with the mind of Christ "who, though he was in the
form of God, did not take equality with God as thing to be
grasped, but emptied himself, taking the form of a servant" (Phil.
2:6-7).

That is the transformation God would work in all of us. If we
only knew. If we only opened ourselves to Christ's Spirit. Thomas
Merton has a celebrated passage which marked a revelatory moment in his life:

> In Louisville, at the corner of Fourth and Walnut, in the center of
> the shopping district, I was suddenly overwhelmed with the real-
> ization that I loved all those people, that they were mine and I
> theirs, that we could not be alien to one another even though we
> were total strangers. . . . I have the immense joy of being *man,* a
> member of a race in which God Himself became incarnate. As if
> the sorrows and stupidities of the human condition could over-

whelm me, now I realize what we all are. And if only everybody could realize this! But it cannot be explained. There is no way of telling people that they are all walking around shining like the sun.[3]

How do we know this truth? How do we shine? As we turn to the Son.

Notes

1. Georgi; Collange, pp. 84 *ff.* I am following Georgi and Collange in my interpretation of this passage.

2. Nathaniel Hawthorne, "The Great Stone Face" in *The Complete Novels and Selected Tales,* ed. Norman Holmes Pearson (New York: The Modern Library, 1937), p. 1184. The part of the story rarely told is Ernest's humility in response to the declaration. He walked slowly homeward "still hoping that some wiser and better man than himself would by and by appear bearing a resemblance to the Great Stone Face" (1184). If we shine, we know the source.

3. Thomas Merton, *Conjectures of a Guilty Bystander* (New York: Image Books, 1968), pp. 156-157.

8
Treasure in Earthen Vessels: The Gospel and the Church

(4:1-15)

WE HAVE THIS TREASURE IN EARTHEN VESSELS (4:2). It is Paul's way of picturing the gospel and the church. Make no mistake, the treasure is the gospel and the earthen vessel is the church. Sometimes we get that confused.

God has put His treasure in our earthen vessels. The jeweled mysteries of his grace are placed in our clay pots. His divinity shines through our dust. WE HAVE THIS TREASURE IN EARTHEN VESSELS. It is the glorious, sometimes bewildering paradox of our calling. Let us examine it.

I

We begin as Paul begins chapter 4: HAVING THIS MINISTRY BY THE MERCY OF GOD. The treasure of gospel ministry is not ours by benefit of our good behavior or our skills or our wisdom. It is no professional expertise we are qualified to perform once we have graduated with a diploma. It is more vocation than profession. We are *called*, and it is a *gift*.

Paul never stopped being amazed by the grace of it all: on his way to kill Christians, flattened by a blaze of light, confronted by the risen Christ, and called by Christ to be his *apostle!* How could this enemy of Christ be called to be an apostle? It all spelled grace. BY THE MERCY OF GOD. A young man, now a Christian, was a member of a Chicago street gang that had killed a social worker who was trying to help them. Later he said, "I couldn't get it out of my mind: while we were killing him, he was dying for us." Paul never got over it either. The way he put it was that while we were still sinners, Christ died for us (Rom. 5:8).

Our ministry comes by a holy calling, and the calling comes by grace. This is where we start.

II

And since we have this ministry by grace, WE DO NOT LOSE HEART. Now Paul turns to the miracle of our ministry: that as we minister in Christ's name we are being changed. Called by grace, we are empowered by grace. FOR IT IS THE GOD WHO SAID, "LET LIGHT SHINE OUT OF DARKNESS" WHO HAS SHONE IN OUR HEARTS TO GIVE THE LIGHT OF THE KNOWLEDGE OF THE GLORY OF GOD IN THE FACE OF CHRIST (v. 6).

The glory of God which burst upon the creation as light and transfigured Jesus' face now shines in our hearts. And as it does, we are being changed. Darkened hearts are enlightened. Cold hearts are warmed. (As someone said, hell is not fire, it is ice.) By the Spirit we receive renewal of heart. And when the human heart is changed everything important is changed. Can we believe this is possible?

In his story "The Happy Hypocrite," Max Beerbohm tells of a debauched and unvirtuous man named Lord George Hell who fell in love with an innocent and saintly young woman. In order to woo and win her, he donned a mask, covering his bloated, evil features with the mask of a saint. The guise worked, and the two were married. Years later a wicked woman from Lord George Hell's past showed up and sought to expose him for the scoundrel and fake she knew him to be. Confronting him in front of his wife, she dared him to take off his mask. Sadly he took it off and, to their great amazement, discovered that beneath the mask of a saint was now the face of the saint he had become in wearing it.[1]

This is our hope—against all odds and all doubts—that as we follow Christ and "put him on," to use another metaphor Paul employs for the Christian life, he changes us who wear him into his likeness. This is the miracle of our ministry, that as we follow Christ he is changing us into his likeness. Again, by grace.

III

Now Paul sobers the conversation by speaking of the requirements of ministry. WE HAVE RENOUNCED UNDER-

HANDED, DISGRACEFUL WAYS, literally, the hidden things of shame. We who bear the light of God in our hearts give up things that hide in darkness.

Next Paul moves to a discussion of how we handle the Word of God. WE REFUSE TO PRACTICE CUNNING OR TO TAMPER WITH GOD'S WORD. (v. 2). Earlier Paul had spoken of those hucksters of the gospel who sell it like cheap wine on the streets, watering it down to make more profit. We are all tempted to use Scripture to our personal gain. When we practice cunning or tamper with God's Word, we change it to suit our own purposes. This is a warning that applies to all theological persuasions. Conservatives and liberals may battle over how to handle Scripture, but the fundamental issue transcends these theological categories: whether we *use* Scripture for our own devices. Shakespeare didn't need to tell us, we already knew: "the devil can cite Scripture for his purpose." The devil and any of us. The issue concerns *hermeneutics,* the method of interpretation. The real questions are these: Do we stand *above* the text as judges of the text—a hermeneutics of arrogance? Or do we stand beneath the text—a hermeneutics of obedience? Do we "man-handle" the text to make it say what we want it to mean—a hermeneutics of prejudice? Or do we stand before the text as listening partner with God in search of God's truth—a hermeneutics of holy conversation? Do we wave the closed Bible as a sign of our authority as perfect interpreters of the Bible—a hermeneutics of power? Or do we open it and submit to its righteousness and grace—a hermeneutics of servanthood?

There are hucksters galore, and they are of all theological stripes. I have been a student at one of the more liberal and at two of the more conservative seminaries in America. I have seen liberals and conservatives who reverence Scripture, and I have seen liberals and conservatives who TAMPER AND PRACTICE CUNNING with it. The issue is integrity: whether we *listen* to Scripture or *use* it.

People today use the Bible to promote their political opinions and financial welfare. People use the Bible to defend personal immorality and social injustice. Some people use the Bible to excuse their own unrighteousness and to dispense cheap grace to others.

Others use the Bible to baptize their own intolerance and to lay heavy burdens on people. We need a hermeneutics of obedience, of holy conversation, of servanthood if we are to be true servants, true ministers of the Word.

Abraham Heschel, a great Jewish rabbi, went to a famous theological conference and listened to Christian theologians debate for a while about the Bible. He kept quiet, and near the end of the conference he rose and spoke saying:

> It has seemed puzzling to me how greatly attached to the Bible you seem to be and yet how much like pagans you handle it. The great challenge to those of us who would wish to take the Bible seriously is to let it teach us its own essential categories and then for us to think *with* them and not just *about* them. [2]

We need as the church to commit ourselves to serious servanthood to the Scriptures. The great test of interpretation of Augustine was this: does this interpretation of Scripture increase the love of God and neighbor? [3]

IV

Now the apostle moves to the centrality of our preaching. FOR WHAT WE PREACH IS NOT OURSELVES BUT JESUS CHRIST AS LORD. That should be inscribed in every pulpit and carved in every pew. A preacher is as one without authority save the authority of Jesus Christ. We are only guests in this pulpit. If Jesus Christ does not remind us of that, the deacons surely will.

Our only authority is Scripture mediated through the Spirit of Jesus Christ. We do not preach personal experience—that would give us precious few sermons. We do not preach our opinions— they should not interest the preacher long, much less the congregation. We do not preach vaulted human reason or *Reader's Digest* common sense or *Psychology Today* psycho wisdom. We preach Jesus Christ.

There's the story about Leonardo da Vinci painting the *Last Supper* (these da Vinci stories seem to crop up like kudzu in preachers' sermons). When he was painting the table, he took great pains to put a wealth of detail in the two cups on the table. A

friend came into the room, saw the cups and exclaimed about the
beauty of the cups, whereupon da Vinci seized the brush and with
a sweep of the hand painted them out saying, "Not that, that is not
what I want you to see. It is the face. Look at his face." Preachers
need to paint out all that distracts from the face of Christ. That is
the treasure. THE LIGHT OF THE KNOWLEDGE OF THE
GLORY OF GOD IN THE FACE OF CHRIST (v. 6).

So, WE PREACH NOT OURSELVES (v. 5). Robert Funk
said, "When God is silent all we can do is gossip." Apart from the
revelation of God in Scripture and in Christ, all we say from the
pulpit is gossip. The recent fashion of confessional preaching
must beware.[4] Inevitably we preach ourselves—our own appre-
hension of the gospel and how we have been apprehended by the
gospel—but we must be careful not to focus unduly on our experience or personality but on the personhood of Christ. Inevitably
the clay of our pots spatters God's treasure—our own peculiar mix
of health and unhealth, our own prides and fears and prejudices—
but we must know ourselves enough to keep our agendas, conscious or unconscious, from preventing the gospel.

Preaching Christ does not have to do with how many times his
name is repeated in a sermon. It means seeking above all else to
show forth his face, convey his mind, reveal his grace and truth. It
means letting his light illumine and guide all Scripture. In Karl
Barth's study there was a picture of the crucifixion by Grunewald
from the Isenheim altar piece. In the center is the Christ hanging
on the cross. Off to the right stands John the Baptist with his almost too long bony index finger (it looks a foot long) pointing to
the Christ. That is a picture of the preacher and of the church.
FOR WHAT WE PREACH IS NOT OURSELVES BUT CHRIST
JESUS OUR LORD. We point.

This all has to do not only with the preaching of the professionals, "in-church preaching" as David Buttrick calls it. It also has to
do with the "out-church" preaching lay people do, as they go
about their daily lives talking about Christ, witnessing his love in
word and deed, sharing the wondrous deeds of God in history and
in our personal lives.[5] We preach not ourselves, but Jesus Christ as
Lord.

We preach Christ. We point. Herbert Butterfield said at the conclusion of his famous lectures *Christianity and History* that there is only one permanent rock on which to stand amid the sands of history and that rock is Christ. His stirring closing call is this, "Hold to Christ, and for the rest be totally uncommitted."[6]

V

Now we move to the controlling image of the passage. We HAVE THIS TREASURE IN EARTHEN VESSELS. It is not dispassionate theological opinion from Paul. It is at the crux of things. He is under attack. His apostleship is being questioned. The super-apostles of his day, giddy with success, with high Nielson ratings and splendid offerings, are making fun of the apostle Paul for all his apparent weakness. He cannot be an apostle and be so weak. HIS BODILY PRESENCE IS WEAK AND HIS SPEECH IS OF NO ACCOUNT (10:10). He preaches a VEILED GOSPEL (6:3), for many do not respond. (His baptism stats are down.) And look at all his troubles! Could God be blessing him if he has such miseries? Paul enumerates them:

> Five times I have received at the hands of the Jews the forty lashes less one. Three times I have been beaten with rods; once I was stoned. Three times I have been shipwrecked; a night and a day I have been adrift at sea; on frequent journeys, in danger from rivers, danger from robbers, danger from my own people, danger from Gentiles, danger in the city, danger in the wilderness, danger at sea, danger from false brethren; in toil and hardship, through many a sleepless night, in hunger and thirst, often without food, in cold and exposure. And, apart from other things, there is the daily pressure upon me of my anxiety for all the churches (2 Cor. 11:24-28).

Paul is a wreck! The opponents scoff: if that is how God blesses his apostles, no thanks! Surely Paul cannot be an apostle.

In face of the scoffing of the *strong,* Paul admits his *weakness* and says God's treasure is in our weak, crackable clay pots to SHOW THAT THE TRANSCENDENT POWER BELONGS TO GOD AND NOT TO US (4:7). It is through our human frailty that God has to work and does work. This is not to be lamented, however, for it helps us see that the power belongs to God and not to us. We may forget sometimes, but it does. The transcendent power belongs to God, and it shines all the more when we let God work through our weakness.

Paul had hardly been on the comfortable lecture circuit as the apostle to the Gentiles. And his humanity showed plenty of cracks, but this was no denial of the authenticity of Paul's apostleship. That is how God works.

Every time a pastor and a church make a covenant to begin their work together, the air is full of messianic expectations. The romance goes both ways. If the church feels the pastor is the messiah, the pastor feels the church is, if not the kingdom of God, at least Camelot. Before long the church begins to see the chinks in the pastor's armor and the pastor begins to see Camelot tarnish a bit. The people will say, "Well, the pastor's human after all." And the pastor returns the judgment. Then they will laugh together and say, "Well, it's just us humans that God has to work with, so let's roll up our sleeves and get to work." And in the gentle laughter of our common humanness, we shall discover the wondrous truth revealed later in this letter: MY GRACE IS SUFFICIENT FOR YOU; FOR MY STRENGTH IS MADE PERFECT IN WEAKNESS (12:9).

VI

A final word of hope for those who have found that "the world is too strong for us."

> WE ARE AFFLICTED IN EVERY WAY,
>   BUT NOT CRUSHED;
> PERPLEXED,
>   BUT NOT DRIVEN TO DESPAIR;
> PERSECUTED,
>   BUT NOT FORSAKEN;
> STRUCK DOWN,
>   BUT NOT DESTROYED (4:8).

Here is a word that tells us that God will be with us no matter what happens or what our limitations are. And with God we will make it. But it also suggests one last word about our ministry. Ministry, the ministry of Jesus Christ at least, goes where people hurt. You go to the broken places of life and to the broken hearted. The Spirit of the Lord leads us as it led Jesus . . .

> to preach good news to the poor . . . .
> to proclaim release to the captives
>   and recovering of sight to the blind
> to set at liberty those who are oppressed,
> to proclaim the acceptable year of the Lord (Luke 4:18-19).

As we go to them with the Spirit of God, *they* will be able to say with us,

> We are hemmed in
>   but not finished off
> At a loss
>   but not lost
> Hounded
>   but not abandoned
> Down
>   but not out.

The mystery of this power lies in the cross. The sufferings that come our way as we follow become *Christ's* sufferings and as such are redeemed in his resurrection life: ALWAYS CARRYING IN THE BODY THE DEATH OF JESUS, SO THAT THE LIFE OF JESUS MAY ALSO BE MANIFESTED IN OUR BODIES (4:10).

The great preacher W. A. Jones tells of being in the foyer after church when a woman passed by. He asked her, "How are you doing?" She replied, "Well, I'm somewhere between 'Thank you, Jesus,' and 'Lord have mercy.'" Aren't we all! And in the midst of it all we find ourselves

AFFLICTED BUT NOT CRUSHED;
   PERPLEXED, BUT NOT DRIVEN TO DESPAIR;
      PERSECUTED, BUT NOT FORSAKEN;
         STRUCK DOWN, BUT NOT DESTROYED.

Why? Because it is in our earthen vessels that God has placed the treasure of grace.

Notes

1. Found in Frederick Buechner, *Telling the Truth* (New York: Harper & Row, 1977), p. 80.

2. Albert Outler, "Toward a Post-liberal Hermeneutics," *Theology Today,* October 1985, 42:290.

3. Augustine, "Oh Christian Doctrine," *Nicene and Post-Nicene Fathers,* ed. Philip Schaff.

4. See my discussion of "confessional preaching in *Retelling the Biblical Story* (Nashville: Broadman Press, 1985), pp. 155 *ff.*

5. David Buttrick, *Homiletic* (Philadelphia: Fortress Press, 1987), pp. 225 *ff.*

6. Herbert Butterfield, *Christianity and History* (London: Bell and Jones, 1950), p. 146.

9
Rulers or Servants

(4:5; 1:24; 6:4)
with an Excursus on Servant Leadership

Paul is struggling with the super-apostles over the nature of true spiritual leadership. "For what we preach is not ourselves but Jesus Christ as Lord," Paul exclaims, then adds the crucial line, WITH OURSELVES AS YOUR SERVANTS FOR JESUS' SAKE (4:5). Here is not an incidental aside. The super-apostles are strutting their power and tyrannizing the faith of the church. In 1:24, Paul says, NOT THAT WE LORD IT OVER YOUR FAITH; WE WORK WITH YOU FOR YOUR JOY. In 6:4, Paul says, AS SERVANTS WE COMMEND OURSELVES and then proceeds to list the most unlikely set of commendations.

There are two opposite errors at work in our churches and in society today: leaders who refuse to serve and servants who refuse to lead.

One style of leadership is pastor as "ruler." A noted pastor once said: "A laity-led, layman-led, deacon-led church will be a weak church anywhere. . . . The pastor is the ruler of the church. There is no other thing than that in the Bible."[1] The authority of the pastor over the congregation is in vogue in some quarters today. The pastor unctiously and humbly calls himself the "under-shepherd" of the church, a title which can be a pious cover for becoming the tyrannical over-shepherd of Christ's flock.

The other extreme is the servant who refuses to lead. In the name of equality and service, pastors refuse to do what they are called to do, lead as "first among equals." Ernest Campbell took on the leader-less pastor in a commencement address at Princeton Seminary and reminded the graduates: "They Also Serve Who Lead."[2] And he offered a new beatitude: "Blessed are those who fulfill the positions that they occupy." Pastors are called, among other things, to *lead*.

But they are *servants* who lead. Jesus is the example, who in face of his disciples' squabbling over who was the greatest took a towel and washed feet. And Jesus said to James and John who were kingdom-climbing upward toward his right and left hands:

> You know that those who are supposed to rule over the Gentiles *lord it over* them. . . . But it shall *not* be so among you; but whoever would be great among you must be your servant, and whoever would be first among you must be slave of all (Mark 10:42-44).

And Peter said, "Tend the flock of God, . . . *not as domineering* over those in your charge" (1 Pet. 5:2-3, author's italics). And Paul says, NOT THAT WE LORD IT OVER YOUR FAITH FOR WE ARE YOUR SERVANTS FOR JESUS' SAKE.

There was, to use the phrase of Hans Kung, this "downward bent" in Jesus' style, and our leadership will have this downward bent.[3] We who lead must take the towel too. The true leader of God's people and any people is a servant-leader. The servant-leader works WITH God's people not OVER them. The servant-leader works for the people's JOY, not their submission. The servant-leader respects the FAITH of the people.

Here is the heart of the unfinished dimension of the Reformation called the priesthood of all believers. Here is the oft-forgotten touchstone of baptist (intentional lower case) doctrine: soul competency and soul-freedom.[4] Do pastors really believe that every soul in the congregation is competent to read and interpret Scripture and to discern what the Spirit of the Lord is saying? Does the pastor believe that the Spirit of the Lord is poured out on all flesh, or only upon the pastor who alone hears the voice of Christ and who alone is the vessel of the Spirit? If the Spirit is available to all, if the soul is competent, then is the pastor willing to give the individual members the freedom to interpret Scripture?

Here is also the cornerstone of what baptists call local church autonomy, the belief that the people of God gathered in local congregations are competent to interpret Scripture and make responsible decisions concerning their common life and faith. And if competent they should be free from any higher human authority, whether pastor, presbytery, or pope. Does the pastor trust the congregation to make sound decisions? We must trust them and enable and equip them to make their congregation as faithful a body of Christ as possible. If pastors do, they are saying something crucial: the church belongs not to the pastor but to the Christ.

At Corinth the traveling missionaries Paul called SUPER-APOSTLES were strutting their power and the people were falling in line. They were tyrannizing their faith, living off their money, and demanding their allegiance. Paul later would wonder why they would put up with one who MAKES SLAVES OF YOU, OR PREYS UPON YOU, OR TAKES ADVANTAGE OF YOU, OR PUTS ON AIRS, OR STRIKES YOU IN THE FACE (11:20). In contrast, Paul says WE WERE TOO WEAK FOR THAT (v. 21). In contrast to these ruler-leaders Paul says WE ARE your SERVANTS FOR JESUS' SAKE (4:5).

Notes

1. W. A. Criswell, *Western Recorder,* March 11, 1986, p. 7.

2. Ernest T. Campbell, "They Also Serve Who Lead," *The Princeton Seminary Bulletin,* New Series, vol. 2, no. 1, 1978, pp. 3-8.

3. Cited in ibid., p. 4.

4. I like James William McClendon's decision to use the lower case *b* when he describes the free church or believers church in the anabaptist/ English baptist historical continuum. I will do the same. It represents the antiauthoritarian and institutionally modest character of the baptist tradition. See McClendon, *Ethics: Systematic Theology,* (Nashville: Abingdon Press, 1986) vol. 1. For exposition of soul freedom and soul competence, see E. Y. Mullins, *The Axioms of Religion: A New Interpretation of Baptist Faith* (Philadelphia: The Griffith and Rowland Press, 1908), especially Chapters 4 and 6; and E. Y. Mullins and H. W. Tribble, *The Baptist Faith* (Nashville: Convention Press, 1935), chapters 2, 4, 5, and 6.

Servant Leadership: An Excursus

It is generally bemoaned that America is in a leadership crisis. Where have all the leaders gone? We also have a followship crisis. If ours is a leaderless age, it is also an antileader age—with good reason. People have stopped following *anybody* because they have been burned by leaders bent on domination rather than service. Haven't we all grown a little cynical in the past twenty or so years? An interesting generation gap in our nation is between those whose basic attitudes about leadership and institutions were formed before the mid 1960s and since the mid 1960s.

Our nation and our churches need a new breed of leaders: leaders who are servants and servants who are leaders. Life in community is a dance in which we need to learn over and over again how to lead and how to follow. If we learn this, maybe our churches, communities, and institutions will move in a graceful waltz; if not, we will continue in an unseemly tug-of-war with bruised egos and bruised toes.

I

The apostle Paul struggled with leadership style in 2 Corinthians. His leadership style and that of the SUPER-APOSTLES were very different. But the issue was there with Peter, too, whom Jesus called to "feed my sheep" (John 21:17). Later Peter reflected on the kinds of leadership shepherds were supposed to exercise with their flock and spoke these words:

> Tend the flock of God that is your charge, not by constraint but willingly, not for shameful gain but eagerly, not as domineering over those in your charge but being examples to the flock. And when the chief Shepherd is manifested, you will obtain the unfading crown of glory. (1 Peter 5:2-4).

Leadership style was a crucial issue for New Testament churches as for us. And it is crucial for all communities and organizations, institutions and nations. Servant-leaders are needed in all areas of life. In this chapter I want to do more than say we ought to be servant-leaders; that is true enough, but is by now a cliche (which someone defined as "a truth that is no longer fun to say"). The biblical defense of such leadership has been offered in Chapter 9, "Rulers or Servants." In this excursus I want to describe servant-leadership. First a story, then the description.

II

The story comes from Hermann Hesse's *Journey to the East*. In the story we see a band of travelers on a journey. Among the group is a man named Leo who accompanies the party as a servant doing menial chores, but he also sustains the group with his spirit and song. All goes well on the journey until Leo disappears. Then the group falls into chaos and the journey is abandoned. Without Leo's remarkable presence they couldn't make it.

The narrator of the story, who was one of the party, after years of wandering finds Leo and is invited to become a part of the Order that had sponsored the journey. When he enters this prestigious group, he discovers, much to his surprise, that Leo, whom he had known as servant, was in fact the head of the whole Order, "its guiding spirit and noble leader."[1]

This intriguing story makes us ponder the nature of true leadership. Are the great leaders not also servants?

III

The cultural mold for leadership is the singularly powerful CEO, Chief Executive Officer. The pastor is often forced into this mold or judged by it. Pastors, as presidential candidates, must defend themselves against "the wimp factor." But American culture has it all wrong today. The issue is not between CEO and Wimp. It is between leadership that in its rulership refuses to serve and a true leadership that *serves*. I will argue that servant-leadership is not only good for the church but also for our world. The biblical defense is in. Now I move to a description of servant-leadership.

I have been greatly helped in my definition of servant-leadership by a man named Robert K. Greenleaf, a management consultant for AT&T, teacher and author, whose book *Servant Leadership* argues for servant-leadership in all areas of institutional life and defines what it means. He begins with a new moral principle for our antileader age: "The only authority deserving one's allegiance is that which is freely and knowingly granted by the led to the leader in response to, and in proportion to, the clearly evident servant stature of the leader."[2] He says that we will freely respond only to leaders who have proven themselves as servants.

A servant-leader is a person who by nature is a servant first, who wants to serve and only later makes the conscious choice to lead. Such a person is "sharply" different from the person who is a leader first and only later may choose to serve once in power.[3]

Woe to any pastor whose first love is to wield authority, for to such does not belong the kingdom. And "woer" still the poor congregation who gets stuck with such a pastor!

According to Greenleaf, the best test of servant-leadership is this:

> Do those served grow as persons? Do they, *while being served,* become healthier, wiser, freer, more autonomous, more likely themselves to become servants? *And,* what is the effect on the least privileged in society; will they benefit, or, at least, not be further deprived.[4]

What a superb test for leadership: (1) Do those being served *grow;* and (2) Are the least privileged of the group benefitted? Is not this what Paul was getting at when he said, NOT THAT WE LORD IT OVER YOUR FAITH; WE WORK WITH YOU FOR YOUR JOY (1:24). Our joy increases as we grow healthier, freer, wiser, and as our least privileged begin to thrive.

Our churches and communities, our institutions and nation, need a new generation of leaders who lead with these goals in mind.

IV

How, then, does a servant-leader lead to accomplish such goals? Greenleaf describes many of the qualities servant-leaders have.[5] I will pick ten and (modestly) call them Ten Commandments for Servant-Leadership:

Thou shalt practice listening and understanding. The servant-leader *listens first,* respecting the people being served enough to listen, to value their insights, wants and needs and to understand, really understand, what they are saying. Francis of Assissi's prayer should apply to all who wish to lead: "Lord, grant that I not seek so much to be understood as to understand."

Thou shalt practice the art of creative withdrawal. A leader needs to take the time and space to withdraw, to see the facts at some distance, a time to ponder and reorient. Optimum performance needs the pacing of creative withdrawal.

A man named Roger Fisher wanted an appointment with John McNaughton, then the Assistant Secretary of Defense for International Security Affairs. Fisher wanted to see him the next day about an important policy issue. McNaughton protested that his day was completely booked up, but after some insistence on Fisher's part invited him to have lunch with him in his office. Fisher was to arrive at 12:35 and be out by 1:15.

Fisher arrived shortly before 12:30. Beside him waited a man who went in at 12:30 and was out at 12:35 with a signed paper in his hand.

Fisher observed this and when he walked in the office he began to criticize McNaughton for the split-second efficiency with which he ran the office. The country was looking for him to think carefully through huge issues, like the one Fisher himself was bringing. How could he do his job at such a feverish pace? And what was so important that McNaughton had to excuse him promptly at 1:15?!

McNaughton smiled. He picked up his calendar and showed it to Fisher. From 1:15 to 5:15 there were no appointments. The four hours were bracketed with the note: *No Appointments—No Interruptions. Think Through. . . .*

Here was one of the keenest minds and most productive public servants America had in the 1960s. Two weeks ahead he had blocked out four hours to think.

Servant-leaders learn the art of creative withdrawal.

Thou shalt offer acceptance and empathy. Acceptance is receiving what others have to say; empathy is projecting yourself in their shoes. Both qualities are the opposite of rejection.

Thou better have intuition. A feel for patterns as they develop and wisdom to know when to act on these hunches.

Thou shalt develop foresight. This is what Greenleaf calls "the central ethic of leadership." He says that the failure or refusal of a leader to foresee is an ethical failure because it is "the result of a failure to make the effort at an earlier date to foresee today's events and to take the right action when there was freedom to act."[6]

A leader must act with eyes to the future and act when actions can make a difference. Anyone can see problems when they are obvious, but by then action to prevent destructive consequences are too late. It is an ethical failure not to give sufficient energy to foresight and prevention.

Thou shalt maintain awareness and perception. William Blake said, "If the doors of perception were cleansed, everything will appear to man as it is, infinite." Leaders must keep the doors of perception open so that they can take in and process all the signals, information, facts that they need. Often fatigue or fear, fear of failure, fear of others, put blinders on us and we limit our perceptions. The good leader faces the future with enough confidence, compassion, and personal health to let in a wide range of data. When you start shutting out important data, you no longer can lead.

Thou shalt value and practice the art of persuasion—sometimes one person at a time. A servant-leader trusts in the noble art of persuasion, very different from the ruler-leader who depends upon coercion. Persuasion is an invaluable resource. It is the method of leadership which values the people being served. Coercion has contempt for people. It says, persuasion will not work with these people, or, persuasion takes too long. Persuasion believes in the good capacities of people who will respond to noble argument well made.

And sometimes persuasion can only happen one at a time. John Woolman, famous Quaker leader, almost single-handedly persuaded the Quakers to give up slavery. One hundred years before the Civil War, Quakers no longer held slaves. He accomplished his mission by journeying all over the countryside visiting homes with slaves and persuading the owners one by one.

Thou shalt accomplish one action at a time—the way some great things get done. We get grandiose and try to accomplish everything at once. This leads to failure and despair. All things, even great things, get done one piece at a time.

Thomas Jefferson was asked to give his energy to the Revolutionary War effort. He knew who he was, however, and the contribution he could best make. He refused those requests, went back to Virginia and, over the course of the next few years, drafted 150 statutes for the Virginia legislature, fifty of which were adopted and became the foundation of the U.S. Constitution.

Thou shalt have gifts of conceptualization. This is the ability to conceptualize ideas and programs which can serve the people.

Greenleaf tells of Nikolai Grundtvig who played a major role in the revitalization of the Danish people. Grundtvig conceptualized the idea of the Danish Folk High Schools, a set of schools which transformed an uneducated peasant class into a vibrant middle class which took the lead in the nation. It all began with a great idea. Ideas do change things, if they are the right ideas and if they serve the people.

Thou Shalt Be Willing to Serve as a "First among Equals." Greenleaf traces the problems in organizations today as coming from two problem areas: (1) trustees who do not take their trusteeship seriously and give over too much responsibility to the officers of the organization, and (2) the concept of CEO as a lone chief atop a pyramid which he says is "abnormal and corrupting."

Greenleaf calls for boards of trustees to take seriously their responsibility and for the CEO to be a *primus inter pares,* first among equals, rather than "lone chief." The faulty CEO leadership structure is diagrammed like this.

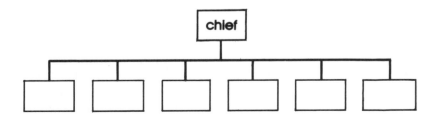

The better structure of the *primus inter pares,* or first among equals, looks like this.

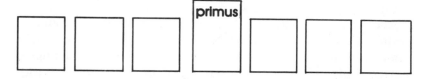

In this second structure the principal leader is not a lone chief making decisions in isolation based on information handed him, but is the leader of a leadership team. Greenleaf's vision for the church follows his vision for all institutions:

> [Building] a society of equals in which there is strong lay leadership in a trustee board with a chairman functioning as *primus inter pares,* and with the pastor functioning as *primus inter pares* for the many who do the work of the church.[8]

A deacon board must learn, as the pastor, to serve as "first among equals." This means that they, along with the pastor, exhibit the ten qualities just reviewed. If so, they will avoid being a rulership oriented board of directors; if so, they will avoid giving up their responsibility to an autocratic pastor; and if so, they will take seriously their calling to serve and lead the church as *diakonoi,* deacons, servants, literally, those who "go through the dust," as a waiter serving tables, a servant washing feet, like Jesus was a *diakonos.*

In the kingdom, the "first among equals" has the spirit of a *last* among equals, last as in *servant.*

V

Those are ten qualities of servant-leadership. Our churches, our communities, and our nation need such leaders; they need to demand such qualities in their leaders.

What is our main enemy today? asks Greenleaf. Not evil people or stupid people or apathetic people or, even, "the system." "The enemy is the strong natural servants who have the potential to lead but do not lead, or who choose to follow a non-servant."[9]

Jesus calls us to serve, but remember, "they also serve who lead," at least that is true for those who lead as servants. So if you wish to serve people, do not be afraid to lead. It will only do us harm if the natural servants leave the leading to ruler-leaders.

And Jesus also calls the church to be a servant-institution, an institution with Jesus' "downward bent," seeking to serve our community and our world. As servants of Jesus Christ and in the service of his love we move into the world in service to the world. And one of our greatest services would be to grow a generation of servant-leaders for our community and world.

Notes

1. This story follows Greenleaf's summary of it in Robert K. Greenleaf, *Servant Leadership: A Journey into the Nature of Legitimate Power and Greatness* (New York: Paulist Press, 1977), p.7.

2. Ibid., p. 10.

3. Ibid., p. 14.

4. Ibid., pp. 13-14.

5. Ibid., pp. 13-48.

6. Ibid., p. 26

7. Ibid., p. 62.

8. Ibid., p. 81.

9. Ibid., p. 45.

10
The Earthly and the Eternal
(4:16 to 5:10)

It is not easy, says Joyce Cary, to paint the new creation on the wall of a condemned building.[1] But this is exactly the witness of those who follow Christ: here in this condemned building the new creation is being formed. How can this be: a new creation happening in this earthly body with all its limitations and weaknesses and with its sure end of death? The answer is given to those who WALK BY FAITH, NOT BY SIGHT (5:7).

People of faith see not only with the outer eye of the body but, more crucially, with the inner eye of the heart. With such vision we can see what is really at work in the world and look forward to the final redemption of our personhood in the eternal house of God.

Paul raises for the Corinthians an important set of questions by way of a stunning set of contrasts.[2] The Christian must choose what is ultimately important. In this choice, in this crisis of decision, is the revealing of the daughters and sons of God.

The SEEN vs. the UNSEEN. Do we live by THINGS THAT ARE SEEN or by the THINGS THAT ARE NOT SEEN? (4:18). By what is or what is to come? Paul is obviously not yet enjoying all the fruits of faith. He has not escaped suffering illness or defeat, and death is sure to come his way. In their human insecurity Christians are always tempted to judge their faith by *present* experience. The opponents of this faith are odd bedfellows: atheists and super-apostles. Unbelievers see only with the physical eye and judge faith by empirical results. And super-apostles abound in every age to promote glorious results *now* and to say, like Reverend Ike put in a New York City ad: "You've heard of the pie in the sky by and by. Get yours with ice cream on top *now!*" (He would also advertise how many Cadillacs were in his church parking lot on Sunday morning.)

THE OUTER NATURE vs. THE INNER NATURE. Will we live by the inner person, the true self shaped in the image of Christ, or by the outer self, the false self, the *persona* shaped by the world? (v. 16).

SLIGHT MOMENTARY AFFLICTION vs. the ETERNAL WEIGHT OF GLORY. Can we endure these earthly tribulations for the sake of a GLORY BEYOND ALL COMPARISON? (v. 17).

The TRANSIENT vs. the ETERNAL. Are we willing to treat what is passing as passing to keep what is lasting? (v. 18).

The EARTHLY TENT . . . MADE WITH HANDS vs. A BUILDING FROM GOD . . . ETERNAL IN THE HEAVENS. Are we willing to rent rather than buy this earthly tent so that we can inherit an eternal dwelling place with God? Are we willing to hold lightly to what is seen so that we can inherit, now in part then in full, the wonderful gifts of the unseen—love, joy, peace in the Spirit? (5:1).

CLOTHED vs. UNCLOTHED. Are we willing to put on the clothes that last, the clothes of Christ (a favorite metaphor of the Christian life for Paul—see Eph. 4:20 *ff.*), rather than the passing duds of the current fashions? We have this choice: to put on the clothes of Christ which is the development of the inner person shaped in Christ's image (his clothes always fit), or, to parade the outer person around in the clothes that are passing away (not only ill-fitting but soon faddishly obsolete) (5:4).

Now in this life we are clothed with God's Spirit, which is the Holy Spirit with its gifts and fruits, which is the Spirit of Christ with its servant love poured into our hearts. If we are now clothed in the Spirit, in the world to come we will not BE FOUND NAKED but will be FURTHER CLOTHED. The Spirit's clothes now are just a preview of things to come and a GUARANTEE of that life to come.

WHAT IS MORTAL vs. being SWALLOWED UP BY LIFE. What a startling phrase; usually we think of being swallowed up by death! Are we willing to face our mortality with realism and Christian hope so that we can really live in this life and look forward to eternal life to come? Unless we are well prepared to die we are ill prepared to live (5:4).

Those are the contrasts. The choices we make reveal who we are and who we are becoming. They tell us whether we are only dying or whether we are also being swallowed up by life. They tell us whether WE WALK BY FAITH (by the inner eye of the heart being renewed in the Spirit) or BY SIGHT (the outer eye of the body enslaved by what is seen).

We are strange creatures, made of earth's clay enlivened with heaven's breath. Clay and spark, earthbound but with a hope of the eternal in our hearts. God has placed in our hearts a great hope: the promise of the kingdom of God.

The spirit of every human person is endowed with longing for heaven. Is such a longing a remembrance of Eden's earlier communion with God still coded in our genes, or in the collective memory of the race? Is it the image of Christ emblazoned on our souls which makes us forever restless with what we find on this earth? Has God placed in our mortal hearts "intimations of immortality," glimpses of heaven even on this earth, which never let us completely resign ourselves to the way things are and keep us longing for the City of God? Has God given us glimpses of the unseen so that we do not become enslaved to the seen? As a lost child hunting a parent's face and never giving up, such is our faith, for WE WALK BY FAITH NOT BY SIGHT (5:7).

This passage is filled with the longing for the eternal. Listen: HERE INDEED WE GROAN AND LONG . . . . WE SIGH (5:2-4) with the longing for the eternal in the midst of earth. Sitting in the midst of earth we long for eternal things.

The church that has stopped longing, sighing, groaning is the church that has lost sight of the eternal; it is the church that has traded in the kingdom of God for the kingdoms of this world; it is the church that has grown so accustomed to the dark that it has forgotten the light. There is more real faith in the groaning of black spirituals than in the easy jingle of *"Victory in Jesus"* (though there's a way to sing *"Victory in Jesus"* with wonder and longing). The church must never be too much at home in the world, for there is a better world and a truer home coming, coming even now in the presence of the Spirit, but always only a GUARANTEE, an "earnest" of better things to come, an appetizer of full banquet table of the kingdom of God.

Men and women throughout the ages have sensed, to use Thomas Wolfe's words,

> a land more kind than home,
> more large than earth.[3]

They have felt a God-shaped void and suffered a cosmic homesickness. They have glimpsed the kingdom-home in Jesus; and this vision has at the same time set their faces toward a final home and thrust them back into the world to make it more like that final realm of justice, joy, and eternal rest.

My most remarkable experience of faith's longing came at Grady Nutt's memorial service at Crescent Hill Baptist Church. Our grief was terrible. Grady was a larger-than-life gift of life and an extraordinary sign of God's goodness, so his death in an airplane crash was an existential crisis (if he is dead, we *all* can die) and also a theological crisis (how could such a good man go down in a plane in the prime of his life?). When his service began, the sanctuary was packed to overflowing with family and friends, lifelong friends, ministry friends, "Hee Haw" friends, and the grieving Crescent Hill, Southern Baptist Seminary, and Louisville communities. We were celebrating the goodness of his life and were weeping an almost unconsolable loss.

Darrell Adams walked to the pulpit and began to sing,

> There's a land that is fairer than day,
> And by faith we can see it afar.
> For the Father waits over the way
> To prepare us a dwelling place there.

It was a voice simple and true, sad and sweet, filled with longing and with a strange hint of joy. Everything got still. All you could hear was his voice and the sound of tears streaming down cheeks. Then he began the chorus,

> In the sweet by and by, . . .
> We shall meet on that beautiful shore.

One voice, Roy Acuff's, began to sing along, then another voice joined, soon the whole congregation was singing in plaintive, sad, and sweet harmony, "In the sweet by and by, we shall meet on that beautiful shore." We were singing for Grady and for ourselves; we were longing for him and we were singing resurrection hope with all our hearts. We were "faithing" that the God good enough to give us Grady would be good enough to give us a place of heavenly reunion, a place where we could meet him and all those others we've loved, or tried to, and find the healing with God and with others only possible in the mystery of the resurrection.

> We shall sing on that beautiful shore
> The melodious songs of the blest,
> And our spirits will sorrow no more,
> Not a sigh for the blessing of rest.

Now we sigh, now we long and walk by faith not by sight; but then we shall see God face to face and understand, finally understand, as we are now understood by God. That's why we Christians are sad and joyful, filled and empty all at the same time. We're earthly creatures touched with the eternal, and on our way there.

Notes

1. Cited in David Buttrick, *Preaching Jesus Christ,* (Philadelphia: Fortress Press, 1988), p. 14.

2. Furnish, p. 288.

3. Thomas Wolfe, *You Can't Go Home Again* cited in *The Questing Spirit,* ed. Halford Luccock and Frances Bientaro (New York, Coward-McCann, Inc., 1947), p. 711.

11

The New Way
of Knowing/Seeing/Living
From *Sarx* (Flesh) to *Stauron* (Cross)

(5:11-21)

Paul continues the defense of his apostleship and the definition of true ministry. He is having to commend himself again (how he hates that) so that the Corinthians can have an answer for those who PRIDE THEMSELVES ON A MAN'S POSITION AND NOT ON HIS HEART. Paul is defining what true transformation and true ministry is about.

FOR IF WE ARE BESIDE OURSELVES, IT IS FOR GOD; IF WE ARE IN OUR RIGHT MIND IT IS FOR YOU (vv. 12-13). Paul may well be countering the arguments of false apostles who prove their spiritual authority by ecstatic experiences (they act "beside themselves"). Paul says: If I have an ecstatic experience it is for me and my God in our relationship with one another; it is not for public consumption and it really does not help you. If I am sober-minded, or IN MY RIGHT MIND, that *is* for you. The wisdom of a human mind in tune with God's wisdom is a great benefit to the church.

This seems a parallel argument to the tongues debate in 1 Corinthians where Paul does not condemn speaking in tongues and in fact calls it an authentic gift of the Spirit, but where he goes on to say it is for private devotion not public display and cannot be used in worship unless the tongues are also interpreted. Tongues alone do not edify the body: "In church I would rather speak five words with my mind, in order to instruct others, than ten thousand words in a tongue" (1 Cor. 14:19). In 2 Corinthians the issue has moved from factions in the church to competition between apostles. False apostles would use their ecstatic experiences to prove their true spiritual authority. Paul would use the more helpful spiritual gifts of preaching and teaching.

But there is a more compelling contrast at work in this paragraph. It is between living according to the flesh, *kata sarx,* and living according to the cross, *kata stauron* (this contrast was first given me by my New Testament professor, J. Louis Martyn).[1]

The event of Christ has changed everything, how we know, how we see, how we live. The old way of knowing/seeing/living is *kata sarx,* according to the flesh, or as the Revised Standard Version puts it FROM A HUMAN POINT OF VIEW. The new way of knowing/seeing/living is *kata stauron,* according to the cross.

New life in Christ means that FROM NOW ON, THERE-FORE, WE REGARD NO ONE FROM A HUMAN POINT OF VIEW (v. 16). Because of what God has done in Christ we do not look at the world the same old way.

The old way, *kata sarx,* is the weary way of looking at the world through the lenses of self-interest. We look at the world as if it is there to serve us. That way of seeing is killing us and destroying our world. We need a new way of looking at the world. The old way is not working.

The old way divides us by race and sex, by class and creed, by beautiful and ugly, rich and poor, educated and not, communist and capitalist, conservative and liberal. And with every discrimination we make, *we* are always on the good side of the equation. *Kata sarx.* But IF GOD WAS IN CHRIST RECONCILING THE WORLD, (v. 19), how can we divide it up again? We need a new way of seeing.

Kata sarx is an endless circle of self-interest. Instead of glasses with clear lenses we wear glasses with mirrors turned inside. All we see is *me.* "The Education of David Stockman" taught Stockman that. No matter how hard he tried as federal budget director to cut the budget, the pressure of self-interest politics won out. In his words, "The hogs were . . . feeding. The greed level . . . just got out of control."[2]

We need a new way of seeing—like that of the woman doctor on the 6 o'clock news. She stood in a Beirut hospital holding a five-month old dead baby. As the reporter stuck the mike in her face, she said, "You tell me that Israel is safer because this five-month old child is dead?!"

We need a new way of seeing. We regard people from human standards and turn God's earth into "killing fields." A girl commits suicide because she cannot look like a model in *Mademoisells*. Catholics and Protestants kill each other in Ireland. We live life completely self-consumed and self-preoccupied and wonder why we are so bored with life.

We need a new way, not *kata sarx* but what? *Kata stauron!* According to the cross. It is seeing the world through Christ's eyes. It is not *kata sarx*, looking at the world as if it is there to serve us, but looking at the world, *kata stauron*, as if we are created and called to serve it.

For Will Campbell it meant loving not only blacks but also his "red-neck" brothers, so he has not only led in the civil rights movement but also befriended Ku Klux Klanners with Christ's friendship. For Mother Teresa it means serving the poor of India. For millions of Christians it has meant an adjustment of life-styles so their lives could help others more.

This new way of seeing has become a new way of living. FOR THE LOVE OF CHRIST CONTROLS US BECAUSE WE ARE CONVINCED THAT ONE HAS DIED FOR ALL (5:14). T. R. Glover said that four short words destroyed slavery: "For whom Christ died." And those words continue to break down every barrier that separates, hurts, destroys.

Paul goes on to describe more fully this kind of love, and we see that it takes on the form of a servant.

AND HE DIED FOR ALL, THAT THOSE WHO LIVE MIGHT LIVE NO LONGER FOR THEMSELVES, BUT FOR HIM WHO FOR THEIR SAKE DIED AND WAS RAISED (v. 15).

To live no longer for yourselves but for him: this is *kata stauron*. To live no longer for yourselves but for him and for the world he so loved: this is no longer *kata sarx* but *kata stauron*.

All this is hardly glamorous; it is far from easy. It runs against the cultural moods and trends. Tom Wolfe called the 1960s the *Now Decade;* he called the 1970s the *Me Decade,* and called the 1980s the *Purple Decade*—the decade of glamor and style over substance. For the Christian every decade is God's time and therefore becomes a *Cross Decade.*

FOR THE LOVE OF CHRIST CONTROLS US. . . . THAT THOSE WHO LIVE LIFE NO LONGER FOR THEMSELVES BUT FOR HIM. . . . FROM NOW ON WE REGARD NO ONE FROM A HUMAN POINT OF VIEW. . . . All these words point to the miracle of the Christian life:

THEREFORE IF ANYONE IS IN CHRIST HE [or she] IS A NEW CREATION (vv. 14-17).

In our world and in us who follow Christ, a new creation is being formed, a new way of knowing/seeing/living. And it is the way of Christ's love that takes the form of a servant.

In Peter Shaffer's award-winning drama *Equus,* the central character, a boy named Alan, has an atheist father named Frank Strang. Strang thinks his son's problems are caused by his religion. In a petulant outburst he speaks to his son about the cross:

An innocent man tortured to death—thorns driven into his head—nails into his hands—a spear jammed through his ribs. It can mark anyone for life, that kind a thing.[3]

We have been marked. This cross, however, is not a sign of death but of life overcoming death. For the love of the living Christ controls us and now we live *kata stauron.* The renewal of the heart by the Spirit of the Lord turns the heart cruciform.

Notes

1. See also these relevant articles by Martyn: "Epistemology at the Turn of the Ages: 2 Corinthians 5:16" in William Farmer, C. F. D. Moule, and R. R. Niebuhr, *Christian History and Interpretation* (Cambridge: Cambridge University Press, 1967), pp. 269-287; and "Focus:

Theological Education or Theological Vocation" in *Callings* ed. James
Y. Holloway and Will D. Campbell (New York: Paulist Press, 1974).

2. William Greider, "The Education of David Stockman," *The Atlantic Monthly,* vol. 248, no. 6, December 1981, p. 51.

3. Peter Shaffer, *Equus* (Middlesex, Eng.: Penguin Books), p. 34.

12
The New Creation Reconciliation

(5:17-20)

The gospel miracle has been announced: THEREFORE, IF ANY ONE IS IN CHRIST, HE [or she] IS A NEW CREATION; THE OLD HAS PASSED AWAY, BEHOLD, THE NEW HAS COME (v. 17). This news captures the ears of our hearts and touches our deepest longing. With Seneca, we want not so much to be bettered as to be transformed. Me, A NEW CREATION! Could it be? Paul is not bashful. As we enter into Christ, we enter into the new creation; as Christ has entered into us, we experience becoming a new creation.

That sounds inviting doesn't it? We're so tired of the old creation, the old way of life, this old tired body, this old confused mind, this old beleaguered heart. Paul announces in the midst of this old creation the dawn of a new creation. Jesus Christ has begun a new humanity. The old humanity of Adam and Eve is being replaced by the new humanity of Jesus Christ.

I

The need for a new creation implies something about the old creation—that something has gone wrong. In the story of our faith and in all our personal stories there is the memory of a good creation and of the experience of a "fall" from that good state into a way of life not nearly so good.

The Garden of Eden is the memory of the human race we cannot erase, a memory of that good work of God epitomized by the word PEACE. The natural world was an unblemished garden. Human relationships were marked by deep communion, nakedness without shame, and loving companionship—and not only between man and woman but also with God, who walked and talked with us in the cool of the day.

Then came what we call the "Fall"—what *The London Times* called the only empirically verifiable doctrine of the Christian faith. Just look around you, read the newspaper, peer into the mirror. Our sin began in distrust of God, moved into disobedience, and landed in discord. From the original peace of the garden we call Eden came the wilderness of warfare, came the age of anxiety, estrangement, and apartheid. We don't have to be persuaded as to the reality of the fall. We know our fallenness, we experience it every hard day, we feel it in our bones.

But as instinctive as is our knowledge of our fallenness, just as deep, deeper really, is our memory of that original peace; for before "original sin" we enjoyed the "original blessing" of God in Eden. We have then an unquenchable thirst for the waters of restoration. We "sigh for Eden." Adam's story is our own:

> He drew the Curse upon the world, and Crackt
> The whole frame with his fall.
> This made him long for home, as loath to stay
> With murmurers, and foes;
> He sigh'd for Eden, and would often say
> Ah! what bright were those?[1]

We yearn to regain what was lost. Feeling alone and apart we long to be at peace again, at home again, to be at one again.

What is this yearning? Is it, to use the poet Aleda Shirley's words,

> a desire for that union
> each of us loses
> in the first months of life
> when the soft sunlight on our cheeks
> and mother and milk are one thing?[2]

Our desire is more, though, than that of reunion with a mother's body. It is to be one with life, one with another, one with God. And the longing is more than psychological yearning for human companionship; it is a spiritual longing for divine companionship. We long for God.

II

So it is with perfect timing that Paul describes the new creation in the next sentence as *reconciliation:* ALL THIS IS FROM GOD WHO THROUGH CHRIST RECONCILED US TO HIMSELF.

RECONCILIATION. That's it. That is our deepest longing: to be at home with God, at home with neighbor, at home with creation, and at home inside our own skins.

GOD WAS IN CHRIST RECONCILING THE WORLD TO HIMSELF (v. 19). Lloyd Pfautsch set his anthem on this text to voice and trumpet. This text demands a trumpet. The devil was once asked what he missed most about heaven, and he replied: "The sound of God's trumpets in the morning." This verse is one of God's morning trumpets.

The new creation and reconciliation belong together—with trumpets. The same trumpets that played on creation's dawn played when God in Christ inaugurated the new creation. Add the solo French horn; this is a "new world symphony" announcing the founding of a new world. Reconciliation is our deepest desire, and reconciliation has happened through Jesus Christ. Fallen creation is restored in him. He is the New Adam, the beginning of the new humanity.

American revolutionary Thomas Paine, flushed with the giddy enthusiasm of all revolutions, said, "We have it in our power to begin the world over again." President Ronald Reagan loved to use that quote, much to the groans of conservatives like George Will ("it would be hard to find," Will says, "a less conservative notion," preferring as all conservatives Old World roots to New World visions). But while some may think this a foolish political notion, New Testament faith has the audacity to say: Jesus Christ is the new Adam. In him we have the power to begin the world over again. He is the new creation and in him we partake of the new creation.

III

The new creation is first the restoration of our relationship with God, the deepest possible reconciliation. And it is not our work. All religions try to win reconciliation by seeking to appease a hos-

tile God. God is mad at us, we say, why else would life turn out
this way? So we have done our religious duties of appeasement.
We've tried to reconcile God to us by smoky sacrifice, acts of
penance, good deeds, perfect attendance, and perfect behavior.
And if things don't get better or feel better, we then become hostile at God. That's why some of the most "religious" people are
deeply hostile to God.[3]

But the gospel of God in Christ is this: God is not a hostile God
needing to be appeased by our good works. Rather, we are invited
to accept a reconciliation already won. Reconciliation is not
something we accomplish. It is God's work. GOD WAS IN
CHRIST RECONCILING THE WORLD TO HIMSELF. The is-
sue is not whether God has changed his mind or whether we have,
as if reconciliation is a change in subjective feeling. Reconciliation is far more; it is God's gracious *act*. It is not that we finally
see what we've never seen before—that God is gracious. It is that
God has acted graciously in Christ to forgive all sins.[4] There is
nothing we can do to earn or to win this reconciliation. All we can
do (or not do) is to receive this gift and live in gratitude. As we do
the new creation begins.

In Christ we begin to experience such transformation. And we
discover that it pertains not only to our relationship to God, but to
everyone and to all creation. Reconciliation gives us new eyes
to see the truth: we are no longer enemies but friends. We take
off our worldly *(sarx)* eyeglasses and put on cross-colored
(stauron) eyeglasses. Our heart is renewed and becomes
cruciform in shape. We take on the love that takes a servant
form.

We begin to see the new creation accomplished in Christ as the
true reality. In Christ the walls of hostility have been broken
down. In Christ there is no Jew or Greek, master or slave, male or
female. Reconciliation! Again, this is not our work, this is the
new creation born into our world and into our lives through Jesus
Christ. Reconciliation. It is the new world transforming our
hearts, our temples, our communities, our families, and our politics.

IV

What a wonder! Has it happened to you? Or, better I should ask, Is it happening to you? "Does it happen all at once . . . or bit by bit?" asked the Velveteen Rabbit. Paul's words make the transformation sound all of a sudden, over in a flash: THE OLD HAS PASSED AWAY, BEHOLD, THE NEW HAS COME (v. 17). Few of us have a "BEHOLD" experience of being suddenly utterly transformed. Do you feel that there is still a lot of the "old" left in you and not nearly enough of the "new?"

Then join a club called *church:* that "assuredly broken yet being-saved" community made up of members themselves broken on the way to being healed.[5] The new creation has begun in us, but it is not yet finished. Super-apostles may pretend to be already perfect and may preach a gospel of instant perfection, but we should know better. Jesus Christ is the New Creation; as we are in him we are a new creation. And in this life that's not always. Paul Tillich writes:

> We only want to show you something we have seen and to tell you something we have heard: That in the midst of the old creation there is a New Creation, and that this New Creation is manifest in Jesus who is called the Christ. . . . We want only to communicate to you an experience we have had that here and there in the world and now and then in ourselves there is a New Creation.[6]

That's it, isn't it? Here and there in our world, now and then in ourselves, the experience of the new creation? Sometimes visible, sometimes hidden, always manifest in Jesus Christ. If you look you can see it. In the sweet embrace of love. When hostilities are overcome and when enemies become friends again. As progress is made in civil rights. At the table of our Lord where all nations and peoples, all races, male and female, well and sick, good and bad alike become one family of God. In that sublime moment when you glimpse Jesus' face and hear God's word of grace and you come home to God and self. The warfare is over. Peace. It happens in those moments when you feel within a sudden unexpected power of goodness, a bit of courage, and a grace to act in ways you never thought possible. Have you ever said, I didn't know that she had it in her, or that I had it in me? That's the new creation. These are evidences, suggestive but far from exhaustive, of the new creation happening here and there, now and then.

Jesus Christ has inaugurated the new creation. Its name is reconciliation. As we enter into him and he into us, we experience this miracle of grace.

Notes

1. Henry Vaughan quoted in William Willimon, *Sighing for Eden* (Nashville: Abingdon Press, 1985), frontpiece.

2. Aleda Shirley, *Chinese Architecture* (Athens, Ga.: University of Georgia Press: 1986).

3. See Paul Tillich, *The New Being* (New York: Charles Scribner's Sons, 1955), pp. 20-22.

4. See Bultmann, pp. 159-160.

5. David Buttrick, *Preaching Jesus Christ* (Philadelphia: Fortress Press, 1988), p. 13.

6. Tillich, p. 18.

13
Atonement:
A Doctrine Better Sung
than Said

(5:17-21)

We are concerned here with the mystery of the atonement. HE DIED FOR ALL. Let me sing you a song of the cross: "When I Survey the Wondrous Cross." Such a hymn is a truer spiritual response than any theological argumentation trying to explain or defend the cross.

The component parts of the word speak the miracle of reconciliation: *at-one-ment*. It is a supreme folly and most tragic irony that Christians fight about the doctrine of atonement. Words like *sacrificial, substitutionary,* and *vicarious* divide us. Divided over the at-one-ment! What we believe about the atonement and how we explain it has often become a litmus test for whether we are true Christians. But how can we explain this mystery? George Buttrick says, "Can we explain the Cross? So far: then faith leaps the rest of the distance, and words are lost in adoration."[1] Maybe if we determined only to sing our doctrine of the atonement, then we could scarcely fight over it. But then we fight over words to hymns, too. But only when we stop singing. So let's keep singing "When I Survey the Wondrous Cross."

Old Testament scholar G. W. Anderson wrote an article entitled, "Israel's Creed: Sung not Signed."[2] A true and living faith is better sung than signed. It is more doxology than legal document. Any people more concerned with signing theological statements than singing them is in danger of losing its own soul.

Above all, let us not fight over theories of the cross. It betrays the reconciliation won at the cross. Make no mistake, Paul connects the reconciliation won with the death of Christ. HE DIED FOR ALL, Paul says (5:15). It is THROUGH CHRIST that we are reconciled (v. 18). And then the mysterious crux of it all: FOR OUR SAKE HE MADE HIM TO BE SIN WHO KNEW NO SIN, SO THAT IN HIM WE MIGHT BECOME THE RIGHTEOUS-NESS OF GOD. (v. 21).

How can we begin to understand? We set our minds to work knowing that they can take us just so far, then faith must leap and words be "lost in wonder, love, and praise."

When we talk of theories of the atonement—ransom, satisfaction, substitutionary, moral influence, etc.—we realize that all are based on human models, worn and contaminated vessels of human thought trying to bear the transcendent light of a love beyond our comprehension. Surely they are EARTHEN VESSELS, and as such all the better through which to see the light—if only we acknowledge that they are earthen and they are vessels. "Sacrificial" theories are based on ritual sacrifice, "ransom" theories based on slave auction blocks, "satisfaction" theories based on law courts, "moral influence" theories based on martyrs' deaths set to music.

All our theories are human; they are contaminated by human ambivalence; they are spattered with human clay, all of which is OK—human words, metaphors, models are all we have to work with—as long as we are wise to peer *through* them to the heart of Divine Love made eloquent in suffering. We do this best in poetry and song, for in these vessels we instinctively know that the words point beyond reason and argumentation, point beyond themselves. In poetry and song we hold our words as bread and wine: holy and fragile vessels of the Divine.

How does Paul say it, sing it? Let's listen. GOD WAS IN CHRIST RECONCILING THE WORLD TO HIMSELF (v. 19).

It all begins with God. God is the initiator of the event of reconciliation and is its primary actor. It is his deed. God is no distant judge waiting for some perfect man to die so that his justice could be satisfied and pardon us. The old preacher's story falls short—the one about the stern teacher about to administer a beating on the puny but guilty pupil when suddenly the strong, handsome student appears to take the punishment for the guilty pupil. This story fails because it ignores the primal truth: God was in Christ.

God himself took on the suffering in the form of the Son. Better imagine a teacher who saves her class from a fire consuming the school building and herself dies in the blaze. Or the story of the sculptor who fashioned his masterpiece in the clay then, fearing the cold night air, wrapped his bedclothes around the statue and in the morning was found dead—from cold.[3] God wrapped himself around us IN Christ.

But that's not all. God was in CHRIST reconciling the world. God initiated the act of redemption, but the agent of reconciliation was Jesus Christ and the instrument of reconciliation was the cross.

The redemption of the word was not trivial—God did not just shrug his shoulders at our sin and say, "Aw, forget about it." Redemption is not distant—God did not send a message by an angel saying, "Something good is going to happen to you." Redemption is close, as close as our human history; it is costly, as costly as a death on a Roman gallows. Redemption is not an idea finally made plain, it is an event, a love poured out on a cross. HE DIED FOR ALL.

But Paul is not through. God was in Christ reconciling THE WORLD. Redemption is at the same time individual and cosmic. It is the most personal of all realities but it embraces all people and all reality. God through Christ reconciled not only US, but THE WORLD. Christ died not only for me but FOR ALL.

At its heart redemption has to do with the forgiving of sin and the withdrawal of divine punishment: NOT COUNTING THEIR TRESPASSES AGAINST THEM. And the forgiving of sin has broken down every wall which separates us and has made us all *one,* at-one with God, at-one with our truest self, at-one with neighbor and at-one with God's created world. From the forgiveness of all sin at the cross has come the new fact of reality: reconciliation.

How has this happened? Somehow, someway at the cross, by way of the death of the one perfect man for all. Now we return to that incomprehensible grace: FOR OUR SAKE HE MADE HIM TO BE SIN WHO KNEW NO SIN, SO THAT IN HIM WE MIGHT BECOME THE RIGHTEOUSNESS OF GOD (v. 21).

How can we explain? How do we understand? Faith leaps and argument turns to song. We put down the sword of reason and poetry becomes our tongue: "When I Survey the Wondrous Cross."

Somehow on the cross an exchange was made, and the universe, "Crackt" by Adam's fall, was healed by the death of the New Adam. In this "happy exchange" (Luther quoting the second-century Epistle to Diognetus), in this "inconceivable exchange" (Barth), Christ became sin so we might become the righteousness of God. As inscrutable as this all seems to our minds we see John the Baptist standing in the Jordan peering at this stranger coming toward him and say with him, "Behold, the Lamb of God who takes away the sins of the world!" (John 1:29). We hear Jesus say something about the son of man who came to give his life as a ransom and wonder over these words till we see him hanging on a cross whose shadow and light still captures the heart of the world.

Is anything more stirring than the sight of a person who gives his or her life for others? "Greater love hath no man than this" said our Lord. The faith proclaims (in song far more poignantly than in argument) that Jesus of Nazareth as the one perfect person and son of God has died for all. And such a death touches the most stubborn of cynics. Even Oscar Wilde, who said:

> There is still something to me almost incredible in the idea of a young Galilean peasant imagining that he could bear on his own shoulders the burden of the entire world . . . not merely imagining this, but actually achieving it, so that all who come into contact with his personality, even though they may neither bow to his altar nor kneel before his priest, in some way find that the ugliness of their sin is taken away, and that the beauty of their sorrow revealed to them.[4]

Whether we are hearing Handel's majestic setting of "Worthy Is the Lamb" or singing "Are you Washed in the Blood," we are witnessing the most important event we've ever known. In the vision from Revelation 7, John glimpsed the saints in white-robed glory and asked how they or any of us could make it through life's testing and tribulation. The angel replied, "They have washed

their robes and made them white in the blood of the Lamb"
(v. 14).

"Are you washed in the blood of the Lamb?" You may wince at
the language or at the foot-thumping self-parodies some "blood
hymns" have become. But we dare not trade in biblical metaphors
for psychological ones. "Unconditional positive regard" cannot
replace the blood of the Lamb. When you are going through life's
bruising and testing tribulation, "I'm OK, You're OK" will not
get you through to the other side.

The blood of the Lamb is our human poetry pointing to the
ineffable self-emptying love of God poured out on the cross. It
points to the truth of grace: what we cannot do for ourselves, God
has done for us! Jesus Christ bore our sins and bore them away.
He was broken on a cross and from his breaking has come our
healing. We cannot wash away the stain of our sins, nor can we rid
the world of its tired and terrible sins, but he is the Lamb which
taketh away the sins of the world.

We may think we don't need that, but the world is filled with
tragic victims of the truth expressed by Myron Madden: *if we
don't accept the atonement, we are doomed to repeat it.* Born
with an undeniable sense of moral justice, most of us believe that
every sin deserves some punishment, and as we sin if we don't
receive just punishment from another, we will find a way to pun-
ish ourselves. Conscious or unconscious guilt will drive us toward
some punishment. But the atonement frees us from the penalty of
sin: ravaging psychological and spiritual death. The voice of guilt
says, You must pay. The voice of grace sings, "Jesus Paid It All."
We, all dying of Adam's blood, are cleansed by the only truly
finally cleansing flood, the blood of the Lamb that taketh away the
sins of the world.

You see, the cross is far more than the *revealing* of the love of
God, though if that were all it would be wondrous enough. On the
cross somehow, someway Christ bore *my* sin, took my place, died
for me. And not only me, for the whole world.

We now live by the inconceivable mercy of God. The cross became the event, cosmic and personal, past and present, where
Jesus became sinful suffering humanity and we became the righ-

teousness of God, his child in whom he takes delight. Glorious
exchange of mercy! God looks at Christ become us and at us who
have become Christ and says, "For you redemption has been won.
Your sins are forgiven."

And we sputter, "How can it be?" and he says, "Look at the
cross." And we say, "How do we know?" and he says, "Look at
the cross." And we say, "What can we do?" and he says, "Nothing, it has all been done!" And we say, "But can't we do anything?" and he says, "Be ye reconciled; simply accept a
forgiveness already won and ever flowing from the cross." And
we say, "Please, isn't there anything we can do?"

And he says, "I give you the MINISTRY OF RECONCILIA-
TION," the *diakonia,* the service of reconciliation. The most
wondrous gift ever given us, reconciliation, now becomes our
ministry. We become servants of its gladness. Minstrels of good
tidings, we get to sing its song. WE ARE AMBASSADORS FOR
CHRIST (v. 20), getting to tell others what God has told us: You
are forgiven, Christ has done it, the walls are broken down, God
is not enemy but friend and now we are all brothers and sisters in
the NEW CREATION. What a song!

> Were the whole realm of nature mine,
> That were a present far too small;
> Love so amazing, so divine,
> Demands my soul, my life, my all.

Notes

1. George Arthur Buttrick, "What Is the Gospel?" *Review and Expositor,* April 1943, 40:160.

2. G. W. Anderson, "Israel's Creed: Sung not Signed," *Scottish
Journal of Theology,* 1962, 16:21 *ff.*

3. Buttrick, p. 159. The story was often used as a metaphor of the
cross by George Buttrick.

4. Ibid.

14

Salvation's Joyful Now: When the Eternal Breaks into Our Time

(6:1-2)

Paul moves from the announcement of the best news ever heard, the new creation of reconciliation, to an appeal: NOW IS THE DAY OF SALVATION! he sings; DO NOT ACCEPT THE GRACE OF GOD IN VAIN, he pleads. These verses deal with the moment when God's eternity breaks into our time, salvation's joyful now.

I

I begin with a personal experience. My wife, Cherrie, and I went walking in Louisville's Seneca Park one Sunday afternoon one fall. It was cloudy and drizzling but that did not deter us; windbreakers on and armed with umbrellas we went. Neither did the cloudiness diminish the beauty of the leaves; rather it seemed oddly to enhance their beauty. The reds, yellows and oranges glowed.

We paused before a meadow wrapped in a crescent of trees. It was the most beautiful sight of autumn color I'd ever seen. The beauty of it all made me dizzy for a moment. We stopped and gazed and then went on. It began to rain harder, the clouds drew closer to the earth, and we pulled our windbreakers tighter as we walked. Five minutes later the weather improved, and we reversed our path. We passed by the same meadow which had made us dizzy with beauty just minutes before. I don't know why, but it wasn't the same, not even close. I don't know whether it was the hard rain or the change in the sunlight or what, but the beauty was faded beyond our comprehension.

We talked about the remarkable difference those minutes had made. What a gift to have passed the meadow just the moment we did. It was an unrepeatable experience of beauty. Had we passed by any other time it would not have been the same. The thought of the giftedness of that moment made us smile and made us thankful.

It is a parable of life and of the mystery of time. The New Testament has two words for time. The first is *chronos,* ticking of the clock time. Tick-tock, tick-tock, measurable, mechanical time. This Sunday, July 16, AD 1989, 3:00 PM.

Then there is *kairos-time,* special time, special moments when something happens that cannot happen again. *Kairos-times* are times of special significance or opportunity, unrepeatable times of beauty or love or holiness which, if we are awake, we can enjoy for all they are worth. *Chronos-time* just ticks along, but *kairos-times* are like the majestic and joyful tolling of bells announcing the gladdest of all days: birthdays, wedding day, Armistice Day, salvation day.

There are moments with friends, moments to love and be loved, moments to enjoy mutual interests and rejoice in each other's company. You must experience them now. Today will soon be tomorrow and the opportunity gone as so many lost yesterdays.

There are moments with children. She will be seven years, one day old just once. We had better enjoy the moments now: the chance to watch a favorite show or talk about seventeen-year cicadas, or share baptism or birthdays.

There are moments with your spouse, moments to be really present to each other, to experience the extraordinary moment of knowing and being known, of understanding and being understood, of loving and being loved. *Now* is when that happens.

And there are *kairos-times* with a church. These may be times of revival and spiritual renewal, they may be times of institutional growth and building programs, they may be moments of mission outreach possible no other time, or moments of ethical crisis when we must take a stand, for example the slavery issue in the last century and the civil rights issue of the mid-twentieth century.

The truly important decisions are made not when everybody has finally agreed on the matter—by then the crucial moment has passed—but in those early moments of crisis when the way is not completely clear.

If we let the *kairos-times* pass, the opportunity is lost forever. Now is the time to decide, to act, to love, to live life to its fullest and best. God provides us special moments of opportunity and decision, *kairos-times,* unrepeatable moments of beauty, love, challenge and holiness. They happen in the now.

II

Paul announces in this text the gladdest *kairos* of all: the joyful now of salvation. Eternity has broken into our time in the uniqueness of Jesus Christ and has brought the salvation we have been waiting for all our lives, and for all our human history: GOD WAS IN CHRIST RECONCILING THE WORLD TO HIMSELF (5:19). The reconciliation of the world! The warfare is over. Peace is won. And not by anything we have done or could ever do, but by what God has done. In Christ. By a grace more amazing than we will ever know.

Salvation has been won! It is done! The majestic bells are joyfully tolling: now, now, now. In the Greek, *nun, nun, nun* (pronounced noon, noon, noon). It is onomatopoeic, the word itself sounds like the tolling of bells.

Paul quotes Isaiah 49 and echoes Jesus:

> At the acceptable time [kairos] I have
> listened to you,
> And helped you on the day of salvation
> Behold now is the acceptable time;
> Behold now is the day of salvation.

The bells are ringing majestically, rolling out the joyful tones for all the world to hear:

Nun, Nun, Nun, .
Now is the time of grace
Now is the hour of favoring

Now is the day of rescue
Today God is restoring ruined lands
Today God is healing desolate places
Today he bids exiles leave their prisons
Today he bids captives come forth to the light.

Today is Good Friday, infinite love poured out, and today is Easter, suffering love become triumphant love.

Now is a time of grace, of God come near, of sins forgiven and wedding party joy and homecoming feasts and Armistice Day parades. The war is over. Reconciliation has been won.

BEHOLD, NOW IS THE ACCEPTABLE TIME.
BEHOLD, NOW IS THE DAY OF SALVATION.

III

And NOW, in the glad urgency of salvation, the apostle says, WE ENTREAT YOU NOT TO ACCEPT THE GRACE OF GOD IN VAIN. In face of such joyous good news, how sad it would be to miss it all. The salvation has been won: this is the *kairos* of the world. But there is another *kairos,* a personal *kairos* for each person when we must accept the grace of God for ourselves. We must not miss this personal *kairos,* so Paul pleads with us NOT TO ACCEPT THE GRACE OF GOD IN VAIN.

How do we accept the grace of God in vain? *We do when we refuse to believe the day of salvation has come,* the warfare over, the peace won, the reconciliation accomplished. Remember the news article a few years back? They found a Japanese soldier in the forest on some South Pacific island, still fighting World War II. He had carried on his guerilla war of survival for twenty or so years after the war was over. When we live as if God has not reconciled us to himself in Christ, as if the peace has not been won, forgiveness given, we accept the grace of God in vain.

Why don't we believe it is done, accomplished, complete? Do you think there is something you must do? Jesus has done it all. All you must do is hear the gladness of the bells and come running. How many of us talk of grace or sing "Amazing Grace" but never believe it for ourselves?

Some other people accept the grace of God in vain by accepting it for themselves, but not being willing to extend it to others. We believe God was reconciling us—indeed we're the kind he wants to be reconciled with—but not the whole world. So we live as strangers and enemies with others, when in fact we now are all children of God, all brothers and sisters in God's family. When peace is only a private thing between us and God and not peace we extend throughout the whole world, it is not true peace and we accept the grace of God in vain. In Jesus' first sermon (Luke 4), in his home church, he read the Isaiah prophecy of the day of salvation and said, "*Now* is the acceptable time, *today* is salvation day" (author's paraphrase). But because he extended God's salvation, God's favor, to all people, his home congregation tried to kill him. If grace is not for all it is not grace, and we accept it in vain.

Some others accept grace in vain by receiving it as the gift of salvation, but then refusing to grow in grace. They refuse to keep on being saved. God is never through saving us, making us more whole, more loving, more like his Son.

If grace is only a thing we accept and not a daily power by which we live, we accept the grace of God in vain. Grace is not a commodity we possess, it is a power by which we are grasped. Grace helps us grow up in Christ, degree by degree being made like him. Such good news. Don't accept such grace in vain.

IV

How often have you heard the word of grace? Have you heard it as unutterably good? Have you accepted it for yourself? Have you accepted its call to speak and live the word of reconciliation in all of life throughout all the world? Have you decided to grow in this grace?

The time to say yes is now. Now is the time to let that grace flood throughout your being, to open every window and every door to its healing light.

Now is the time. Now the *kairos*.
Nun, Nun, Nun!
Now is the hour of favoring.
Now is salvation's day.
Now is the time when grace reigns.

The bells are tolling majestically, joyfully.
Will you respond today, in Salvation's Joyful Now?

15
Will the Real Minister Hobble Up?

(6:1-10)

"Will the real minister please stand up!" was the refrain of the sermon. The text was 2 Corinthians 6:3-10 and the preacher was Nancy Hastings Sehested.[1] Throughout the history of the church there has been disputation concerning who the "real" ministers are. Second Corinthians is an early case study as Paul defends his apostleship against the charges of the super-apostles.

Paul might well have turned the phrase more ironic: "Will the real minister please hobble up!" His own vision of ministry turns the ministry style of his opponents on its head. They are super-apostles unmarked by life's tribulation; they are the wise, the strong, and the healthy. Paul, in contrast, speaks of a suffering apostolate hobbling along in Christ's service; they are the foolish, weak, and wounded.

I

Paul's defense of real ministry takes on a highly ironic cast. Karl Plank's study of Paul's "catalog of adversity" in 1 Corinthians 4:9-13 is most helpful in studying this passage. Do you remember it?

> For I think that God has exhibited us apostles as last of all, like men sentenced to death; because we have become a spectacle to the world, to angels and to men. We are fools for Christ's sake, but you are wise in Christ. We are weak, but you are strong. You are held in honor, but we in disrepute. To the present hour we hunger and thirst, we are ill-clad and buffeted and homeless, and we labor, working with our own hands. When reviled, we bless; when persecuted, we endure; when slandered, we try to conciliate; we have

become, and are now, as the refuse of the world, the offscouring of all things.[2]

That passage and 2 Corinthians 6:3-10 are not the only times Paul catalogues his adversities; read also 2 Corinthians 4:7-10; 11:23-27; 12:10; Romans 8:35; and Philippians 4:11-13. Is Paul just complaining? Is he a hypochondriac or a masochist who enjoys his sufferings and loves talking about them?

No, in these catalogs, as well as other passages, Paul uses the language of affliction as he becomes a "kind of poet." His voice turns to the sad and sweet song of the wounded being redeemed by a crucified and risen Lord. It is the song of a world groaning in travail waiting for the redemption of the children of God, knowing that its sufferings are not worth being compared to the glory that is to come.

Paul's language of affliction reveals his deepest convictions about the nature of reality and the shape of the gospel. Creation is still groaning in travail; it is being redeemed but is not yet fully redeemed. Therefore, God's ministers, themselves being redeemed but not yet fully redeemed, enter into the common weeping as wounded healers.

The super-apostles would paint a black and white world without paradox. Pain and pleasure, failure and success would be easily defined and explained. God has to do with pleasure, success, health, wealth, power, beauty, etc. It is the godless or sinful who encounter the other side of life: suffering, disease, defeat, weakness, etc. In contrast, Paul would speak of a world being redeemed by the gospel in such a way that there is strength *in* weakness, life *in* death, comfort *in* suffering, riches *in* poverty, victory *in* defeat. Paul refuses to see the world in any other way than as it is, a world racked with suffering (he is no Pollyanna Paul), but he also refuses to see God either banished from such a world or assigned to the "winners" only. In Plank's words, Paul's language of affliction is an ironic vision:

> The ironic vision sets the afflicted free not from the existence of suffering, but from the fear of its assigned meaning: the expectation that human plight drives away the presence of God and the

communion of human beings; the dread that in our dying we are alone, cut off from life.[3]

Suffering in life does not mean for Paul that God is dead, absent, or angrily judging us. Suffering is the plight of a world being redeemed but not yet redeemed. And God is with us in such a world, comforting, giving life, fighting evil, and toppling enemies who bring suffering. Therefore, ministers of such a God in such a life enter into the suffering of the world as wounded healers.

People in Corinth, as in all cultures, want a theology of glory, a religion that says God's Spirit will rescue us from all suffering and heal us of all diseases. And it would want ministers, therefore, who manifest the blessing of God in terms of health, wealth, and power. Paul instead talks of his weakness. The *asthen* Greek word group which Paul often uses not only refers to physical illness but also to a kind of weakness in the face of life's onslaught.[4] Nobody wants a sickly asthmatic apostle. The super-apostles have preyed upon the church with such feelings and said that Paul, with all his weakness, cannot be an apostle. Paul defends himself with this highly ironic and provocative picture of the apostle as fool and weakling.

Paul defines real ministry in his own way. He begins, AS SERVANTS OF GOD [not as domineering lords] WE COMMEND OURSELVES IN EVERY WAY (v. 3). Paul's commendation may strike us as very odd. Paul says that ministry is not known by success or failure, but by how we meet success or failure. Our commendation comes by way of OUR STEADFAST ENDURANCE; DISTRESS, HARDSHIPS, AND DIRE STRAITS; FLOGGED, IMPRISONED, MOBBED; OVERWORKED, SLEEPLESS, STARVING (v. 4, NEB).

That's not all. We commend ourselves by the INNOCENCE OF OUR BEHAVIOR—we must act with integrity and without duplicity. And by OUR GRASP OF THE TRUTH—we must hold fast to the truth of the gospel as it has been handed down to us. Contemporary perversions of the gospel always abound. And by PATIENCE AND KINDLINESS. Patience is a companion virtue to hope. Patience does not give up. Patience refused to adopt violent

or coercive or dishonest means in pursuit of our ends. Sometimes
impure means can bring a victory, but we pay later for our unethi-
cal means. Patience is trust in God over the long-haul to win the
victory with pure means. And KINDLINESS—there is no place in
the kingdom for cruelty or rudeness. We can be determined and
insistent and stand firm and still be gentle representatives of the
kingdom. And we are known by GIFTS OF THE HOLY SPIRIT,
by SINCERE LOVE. How terrible that we need to use the adjec-
tive "sincere!" Love is too easily feigned; too often it is eased as a
velvet slipcover over a sledgehammer about to be lowered on our
heads. And we are known BY DECLARING THE TRUTH, BY
THE POWER OF GOD" (v. 6, NEB).

But the POWER OF GOD does not always manifest itself in
instant rescue, healing, and strength. Real ministers cannot be
known by success or failure, health or sickness, but by how we
meet these varying seasons of our lives. For, as Paul says with
unerring realism, HONOR AND DISHONOR, PRAISE AND
BLAME, ARE ALIKE OUR LOT. The real issue is not how we
look in the eyes of the world, but in the eyes of God; it is not how
we are faring in the kingdoms of this world, but in the kingdom of
God. Paul recites a remarkable litany of commendations, the
marks of the true apostolate, a set of beatitudes, actually, beatitudes for the minority band called disciples of Jesus Christ:

> We are the impostors who speak the truth,
>   the unknown men whom all men know;
>   dying we still live on;
>   disciplined by suffering, we are not done to death;
>   in our sorrows we have always cause for joy;
>   poor ourselves, we bring wealth to many;
>   penniless, we own the world
>   (2 Cor. 6:8-10,NEB).

What an odd set of beatitudes, but it is the oddness of the gospel
similarly expressed by our Lord in his beatitudes given in Matthew 5 and Luke 6. True ministry in a world of suffering is not that
of super-apostles but that of the suffering apostolate.

Super-apostles preach a theology of glory and promote a kingdom of the healthy, wealthy, and wise. Christ's suffering aposto-

late preach a theology of the cross and enter a kingdom of the sick, the poor, and the foolish saying that it is precisely there at that cross and in that kingdom that we discover the power and wisdom and healing of God.

Super-apostles would promote ministry through strength. The suffering apostolate speak of ministry in weakness, a weakness that knows the connection between "the passion of Christ" and "the passion of the world," to use the image of Leonardo Boff.[5] The mystery of the passion of Christ and the passion of the world is that life is being generated where death appears.

Super-apostles scorn Paul and all apostles of weakness, but Paul knows better. He has met the crucified and risen Messiah. He knows that ministry is not an escape from the suffering of this world but an entering into its passion as bearers of Christ's grace.

We may look like a motley band of folk to be serving the God of the universe, but we follow the One who took on the form of a slave and became obedient even unto death.

Bishop Desmund Tutu, recipient of the Nobel Peace Prize, says that when we meet the Lord in the life to come he will ask one question: "Where are your wounds?" Paul, for one, will know how to answer.

Notes

1. The sermon was delivered at the pastor's Forum, St. Louis, June, 1987. At that time she had recently resigned as associate pastor of Oakhurst Baptist Church in Atlanta, Georgia, and was soon to be called as pastor of Prescott Memorial Baptist Church in Memphis, Tennessee.

2. Karl A. Plank, *Paul and the Irony of Affliction* (Atlanta: Scholars Press, 1987).

3. Ibid., p. 94.

4. Gerhard Kittle, *Theological Dictionary of the New Testament* (Grand Rapids, Mich.: Wm. B. Eerdmans, 1964), 1:490 *ff*. Plank, pp. 20 *ff*.

5. Leonardo Boff, *Passion of Christ, Passion of the World* (Maryknoll, N.Y.: Orbis Books, 1987).

16
Godly Sorrow and Worldly Sorrow
(7:5-13)

Paul speaks in these verses of two contrasting kinds of sorrow, godly sorrow versus worldly sorrow.[1]

The background for these verses is in 2 Corinthians 2. A brother in the Corinthian church has publicly attacked Paul. He has probably said untrue things in order to undermine Paul's position with the people. Paul has written a letter asking them to discipline this brother. After a painfully long wait, Paul hears that this brother has been disciplined by the church. In turn Paul now urges the church to temper their discipline so that it not be TOO SEVERE: FOR SUCH A ONE THIS PUNISHMENT BY THE MAJORITY IS ENOUGH; SO YOU SHOULD RATHER TURN AND COMFORT, OR HE MAY BE OVERWHELMED BY EXCESSIVE SORROW (2:6-7).

Now later in chapter 7 Paul is thanking the church for their support of him manifested in their discipline of this brother, and he returns to the theme of church discipline. Discipline is always for the purpose of forgiveness and restoration—whether in church or school or family. Inclusion not exclusion is the goal. The church is at the same time a community of morals and mercy. As a community of morals, discipline is necessary for those who flaunt their violation of the values of the community. But because the church is also a community of mercy, grace always our first and last word, discipline is always for the purpose of restoration—the reinclusion of the offending member.

Paul now returns to this theme, speaking not only for the brother but now also to the church which had responded to Paul's letter of complaint and disciplined the brother. His letter had GRIEVED them, but their grief had moved them to proper action: AS IT IS, I REJOICE, NOT BECAUSE YOU WERE GRIEVED BUT BE-CAUSE YOU WERE GRIEVED INTO REPENTING; FOR YOU FELT A GODLY GRIEF. . . . FOR GODLY GRIEF PRO-DUCES A REPENTANCE THAT LEADS TO SALVATION AND BRINGS NO REGRET, BUT WORLDLY GRIEF PRO-DUCES DEATH (7:8-10).

Here is an important and intriguing contrast: GODLY SOR-ROW *(kata theon lupe)* versus WORLDLY SORROW *(tou kosmou lupe)*. GODLY SORROW leads to SALVATION, repentance, healing, and life. WORLDLY SORROW leads to DEATH, de-spair, and destruction.

GODLY SORROW is the spiritual sadness that realizes one has wounded another and thereby wounded the Divine love, the dear-est love in the world. This excruciating pain of the soul feels that one, to use the words of James Denny, "has fallen away from the grace and friendship of God." To feel such sadness is to really grieve, grieve not in a self-consumed, narcissistic, and despairing way, but with a "healing, hopeful sorrow."[2] To grieve in such a way is to know you can change, that your change will make a difference, and that such change will be met with the welcoming mercy of God. Therein it is hopeful.

In contrast we see WORLDLY SORROW. There are two forms of such sorrow. The first is a kind of *insincere sorrow* that is ex-pressed only to coerce a quick forgiveness. Such sorrow does not feel the pain or know the damage that one's actions have caused and so issues a flip apology designed to quickly fix things as if nothing has happened, no injury incurred. Such an apology *ex-pects* forgiveness, as if saying, "I'm sorry" entitles you to for-giveness. We are witnessing a wave of such insincere, worldly sorrow today from preachers to politicians, from judges to gen-erals.

Wise parents learn early on to distinguish worldly and godly sorrow in their children's voices. Children learn that tears may work better than anything else in getting what they want: sympathy or forgiveness or, better yet, getting their tormenting brother or sister in trouble. Wise parents discern the difference between deep, true tears and insincere tears used as a ploy.

But insincere sorrow is not the kind of WORLDLY SORROW Paul is focusing on here. What he has in mind is an *oppressive sorrow* that ladens a person with guilt so that it leaves a person in paralyzing despair. The first kind of WORLDLY SORROW is practiced by the person with no conscience; this kind of sorrow is the plight of the person with a tyrannical conscience, an inner judging voice that never lets them off the hook. It is the kind of conscience more severe than God ever is because God's righteousness is always wrapped in mercy.

Sometimes the church or parents or culture impose such a tyrannical conscience on children. Oft times they prey on people with such tender consciences, knowing guilt is the best method of control. Such WORLDLY SORROW, however, leads to death.

That is why Paul is clear to remind the Corinthians now that discipline has been administered to forgive and comfort the brother lest he be OVERWHELMED WITH EXCESSIVE SOR-ROW. Such excessive sorrow is the WORLDLY SORROW that despairs of forgiveness or restoration and gives up. It does not lead to repentance, healing, and life because it despairs of the possibility of grace.

Many times we practice overkill on our fallen folk, dropping atom bombs of condemnation on the mud huts of their guilt. Why does the church shoot its wounded? Only because we lose sight of our Lord who lived by the deep mercy of God who offered "grace greater than our sin." Paul exclaimed, Sin abounds but grace abounds all the more! (Rom. 5:20) something he never knew until he met the risen Lord.

Remember our Lord of whom it was said: "He will not break a bruised reed or quench a smoldering wick" (Matt. 12:20). Our churches and our world are filled with bruised reeds and smoldering wicks, people overcome with a WORLDLY SORROW leading them to despair and death. It is compassion not condemnation, mercy not criticism that will lead them to the grace of God.

These are the bruised souls who pray with George Herbert in his poem called "Discipline,"

> Throw away Thy rod,
> Throw away Thy wrath:
>   O my God,
> Take the gentle path.
>
> For my heart's desire
> Unto Thine is bent:
>   I aspire
> To a full consent
> . . . .
> Though I fail, I weep.
> Though I halt in pace,
>   Yet I creep
> To the throne of grace.
>
> Then let wrath remove;
> Love will do the deed:
>   For with love
> Stony hearts will bleed.[3]

And our Lord, righteous and merciful, gentle, patient and kind will not break the bruised reed or quench the smoldering wick. He will not lay on us a WORLDLY SORROW that leads to death but will lure us by grace to a repentance that leads to life. Often our religion breaks bruised hearts, but Jesus comes with grace welcome as rain to parched souls.

The contrast of GODLY SORROW and WORLDLY SORROW find their counterparts, their types, in two of Jesus' disciples, Peter and Judas.[4] Peter's GODLY SORROW led to repentance and life, to an encounter with the Risen Lord at the Sea of Tiberius where Peter was restored by grace and called by grace to be a disciple again, to be Peter again; and Judas's WORLDLY SORROW led to despair and death.

Judas betrayed Jesus, leading the soldiers to capture him, betraying him with a kiss. "Hail Master!" he said and kissed him. And Jesus said, "Friend, why are you here?" (Matt. 26:49-50). The great sadness of this story is that Judas didn't wait, couldn't wait for Easter, until Jesus rose and appeared to him. So overcome with WORLDLY SORROW, despairing of any hope of forgiveness and restoration, he killed himself (Matt. 27:5).

The Resurrection appearance that didn't happen. Can you imagine how wonderful it would have been? Grace enough for Peter, grace enough for Judas. Grace enough for denial and enough for betrayal too.

Judas no doubt would have been alone, too ashamed to have made his way back to the rest of the disciples. And this Stranger would have come up behind him and said, "Friend, why are you here?" And Judas would have turned and said, "Master." And Jesus would have said, "Judas, you too are forgiven. You belong with us. Come on, let's go rejoin the rest." How wonderful that would have been.

And this time it would have been Jesus who gave the kiss, not the kiss of death but the kiss of life,[5] and, to use the words of the psalmist, with "lips moist with grace," grace greater than all our sins.

Why did Judas despair of such grace? Why do any of us? We cannot know. It is hid in the mystery of the human mind and held in the mercy of a loving God. This missed opportunity of grace, however, is powerful to turn our minds to Paul's contrast between worldly and godly sorrow. And it should compel us, the church, to be such a people of grace that we not heap worldly sorrow on our bruised reeds of souls lest they despair to see the Savior's kind face.

Notes

1. Denny, p. 255.
2. Ibid., p. 256.
3. George Herbert, "Discipline," *The Country Parson; The Temple,* ed. John N. Wall (New York: Paulist Press, 1981), p. 305.
4. Peter and Judas as types of these two sorrows was mentioned by HCG Moule, p. 74.
5. This image comes from Frederick Buechner, *Peculiar Treasures* (San Francisco: Harper & Row, 1979), p. 83.

17
The Offering:
Grace, Gratitude and Giving

(Ch. 8—9)

What are these two chapters, 8 and 9, doing in the middle of this letter? Right in the middle of his passionate defense of his apostolic ministry, Paul interrupts to pass an offering plate and take up a collection for the poor in Jerusalem.

Some scholars say that these chapters do not belong—that they were stuck in by a later editor. It does seem a bit out of place—like the offering seems out of place in the worship service. "What has this crass collection of cash to do with the beauty of holiness and the worship of God in spirit and in truth?!"

It does seem out of place until we remember that our religion is a religion of grace. *Grace* is the first and last word of our existence as children of God. And there is no receiving of grace without gratitude, and there is no gratitude without giving.

A word of background. Paul had begun a collection for the poor in Jerusalem in his first visit. The offerings had slowed to a trickle. Paul's very request for money on their behalf had become, or would soon itself become, a matter of controversy. Paul here gives a new plea for their generous giving.

I

Paul's plea is consistent with Old Testament faith and the religion of Jesus. Ours is above all a religion of grace. There is a giftedness to all of life. The Old Testament keeps reminding us as it reminded the children of Israel: all of life, this new land, all you have and are is a gift from God. And the warning accompanied the reminder: take heed lest when you are full and healthy and wealthy and live in beautiful houses that you forget it was God

who freed you from slavery and gave you this land. Take heed lest
you say, "My power and the might of my hand has gotten me this
wealth" (Deut. 8:17). The problem with the self-made man, goes
the joke, is that he worships his creator.

Life is gift and all we have and are is grace. Such was the vision
of Jesus. All of life was a gift, the land, the rain, bread, wine,
family, work, friends, and love—all are gifts from our good
Father in heaven.

Jesus' life was a continuous song of thanksgiving. Even in the
face of rejection at the hands of the leaders of the Jews, Jesus
prayed: "I thank thee Father, Lord of heaven and earth, that thou
hast hidden these things from the wise and understanding and revealed them to babes" (Luke 10:31). From the waking of the day
to the breaking of bread, from a wedding feast to a cross, Jesus
lived a life of thanksgiving.

And what Jesus offered was a religion of grace. A startling reversal has happened with Jesus. Repentance and salvation
changed places. Before, under the law, repentance came first as a
prior requirement, a prerequisite for salvation. Now in Jesus salvation takes the initiative. In a religion of grace, salvation does not
wait for our repentance but brings repentance in its healing wings.

Repentance is not the offspring of obligation, it is the child of
gratitude. We change not *in order* to earn God's love; we change
because of God's love.

Salvation has come first in Jesus. "Jesus came . . . preaching,"
Mark's Gospel records, saying, "The time is fulfilled, and the
kingdom of God is at hand; repent, and believe in the gospel"
(Mark 1:14-15). The kingdom has come graciously near in Jesus.
God has taken the first step toward us.

When he encountered persons trapped in sin, he said, "I do not
condemn you, your sins are forgiven, go and sin no more." That
was the pattern of grace. Not, "If you sin no more, I will forgive
you"—that is the law. Not, "Your sins are forgiven, go do as you
please"—that is tolerance. But, "[Your sins are forgiven,] go, and
sin no more" (John 8:11, KJV). Forgiveness comes first, bringing
a repentance not driven by obligation but rather bathed in gratitude.

That pattern of grace was the way Jesus encountered the woman at the well, Mary Magdalene, and the woman caught in adultery.

That was how Jesus encountered Zacchaeus. Jesus didn't say, "Zacchaeus, if you quit your cheating and repay those you have cheated, I'll come have lunch." He just walked up and invited himself to lunch. And the startling initiative of Jesus' acceptance evoked from Zacchaeus works of repentance. Salvation came to that house that day.

Even the conversion of the prodigal son speaks to the priority of grace. As soon as the father saw his son way down the road, he started running toward him. And before the son could spit out his carefully rehearsed speech of repentance, the father embraced him and called for a homecoming feast.

The religion of Jesus is a religion of grace. It did not wait for our getting ready, it did not wait for us to get good enough. "While we were yet sinners, Christ died for us" (Rom. 5:8). Jesus offers the grace of God. God has spoken in Jesus Christ and what He has spoken is not *yes and no*, not *yes, but* or *yes, if,* but always YES (2 Cor. 1:20).

II

That is why when Paul passes the offering plate in Corinth for the poor, his most persuasive argument for giving is *grace*. Grace begets gratitude and gratitude begets giving.

Why do we give? How do we give? The last verse of chapter 9 tells us: THANKS BE TO GOD FOR HIS INEXPRESSIBLE GIFT (v. 15).

And that is how Paul begins too. He tells the Corinthians he wants them to grow in the grace of giving. Giving money is a response to grace and is itself an act of grace. Six times in the first nine verses of chapter 8 Paul uses the word *grace,* sometimes to mean God's act, other times to signify our act. Everything we do and are in Christ is grace.

Paul is concerned about the poor in Jerusalem. His first, last, and best appeal is grace, but he pulls out all the stops, using other appeals as well to pry open their pocket books.

He appeals to their spiritual pride: You have excelled in the other gifts of the Spirit—faith, tongues, knowledge, etc.—now I want you to excel in the spiritual gift of giving, in the grace of generosity (8:7).

Then he uses shame. The Macedonians have given a big offering and they are poor folks themselves. You would look awfully bad if you gave a stingy offering. Besides, I've already bragged on you. Don't let me down (8:1-5; 9:3-5).

Next Paul appeals to their self-interest. He uses a farming illustration: if you sow sparingly, you'll reap sparingly; if you sow bountifully, you'll reap bountifully. We should not give this a crassly materialistic interpretation. God does not reward us tit for tat, dollar for dollar, but he rewards us with a better, fuller way of life. If you sow abundantly, the kingdom of God will yield a bountiful harvest in you (9:6-12).

Next Paul appeals to their trust. Don't be anxious, he says, God is able to take care of you. God will provide more than enough so that you can keep what is enough and keep on giving generously to others. How interesting a theology of stewardship in this verse: God gives you more than enough so that the *more than what is enough* you can give to others (v. 8). Trust the God who blesses and provides, he says. Giving is an act of trust.

This is our worship, too, Paul goes on to argue. Worship is not just pretty words and music offered to God. It is also gifts given to the poor. For your giving, he says, NOT ONLY SUPPLIES THE WANTS OF THE SAINTS BUT ALSO OVERFLOWS IN MANY THANKSGIVINGS TO GOD (v. 12).

So Paul appeals to pride, to shame, to self-interest, to trust, and to worship. But his best and truest appeal is *gratitude*. Grace and gratitude, THANKS BE TO GOD FOR HIS INEXPRESSIBLE GIFT! (v. 15). Look at the grace of our Lord Jesus Christ, who, THOUGH HE WAS RICH, YET FOR YOUR SAKE HE BECAME POOR, SO THAT BY HIS POVERTY YOU MIGHT BECOME RICH (8:9).

Paul closes with doxology. THANKS BE TO GOD FOR HIS INEXPRESSIBLE GIFT, JESUS CHRIST. There aren't enough words or words good enough. There aren't enough deeds or deeds pure enough, there aren't enough songs or songs beautiful enough.

> Were the whole realm of nature mine,
> That were a present far too small.

Such giving is not to be painted in the somber tones of martyrs' deaths, nor in the unhappy drone of duty. As those who give by grace, in grace and as grace, we give freely and joyfully. So Paul says, EACH ONE MUST DO AS HE HAS MADE UP HIS MIND, NOT RELUCTANTLY OR UNDER COMPULSION, FOR GOD LOVES A CHEERFUL GIVER (9:7). The Greek word for *cheerful* is *hilaron,* from which we get the word *hilarious.*

God loves a hilarious giver! Hilarious givers are those who, lured by the extravagant kindness of God, give with their own kind of crazy extravagance, the way lovers give gifts to their beloved. Not counting the cost and with no miserly pinching of pennies, we try to figure out how much we can give rather than how little. And the giving is with no calculation of return; we give *because of,* not *in order* to.

There's an old line about how we should give: "until it hurts." What a dreary formula. Better we should say, "Give until it no longer hurts," or "Do not give out of your pain but out of your joy." Give as those giddy with God's grace give: recklessly, lavishly, hilariously to the God who has so recklessly and extravagantly loved us.

III

How is the Christian to live with regard to possessions? A person came once to me and said, "I've never been able to find some peaceful middle ground between sackcloth and silk!" Is there a way between sackcloth and silk? I think so. In fact, these two represent two ways which lead us astray.

The first way is the dominant cultural voice of affluence. It says: you are what you own. It says: *my* power, *my* hand. It is characterized by a grasping hand, by getting and keeping. What flows into that life stops there, like the water that flows into the Dead Sea stops only to evaporate or turn to salt. It is the way of boredom—the curse of a people blessed who do not follow God's call to be a blessing.

The other way is the countercultural voice of asceticism. If the way of affluence is the silk, this is the sackcloth. It is the negative image of our affluent society. It says you are what you refuse. It is characterized by the hand extended, the palm up in refusal. It calls the blessing of God a curse. It pretends purity. It takes on airs. It wears sackcloth like a socialite wears a Halston gown. It may not be tempted by greed as the way of affluence, but it is riddled with pride.

But there is a third way beyond silk, beyond sackcloth. It is the biblical path of stewardship. Above all voices it hears the voice of Christ, and its way is the way of generosity. It is not silk, it is not sackcloth, it is not even a sensible cloth coat.

The way of Christ is stunningly different. It's hand is not the grasping hand of affluence characterized by getting and keeping. Its hand is not the ascetic palm up in refusal. Its hand is open, joyfully receiving and joyfully giving. It is the way of generosity. It knows "kept grace" is a contradiction in terms. Grace given is always on its way to someone else. It knows that a life which only catches blessing and does not become a channel of blessing ruins the life and spoils the blessing.

This is the way of generosity. It may appear affluent, but its look is altered by a truly generous life-style. It may look modest, but its goal is not to look modest or to look any way but to love God and neighbor.

A miracle has happened to the Christian. The closed circle of getting and keeping has been broken. We become vessels of receiving and giving, channels of blessing.

IV

The Christian way is the way of grace, gratitude, and giving. We are vessels which pour from our fullness into the lives of others. Our life-styles, our budgets, and our gifts of what we have and who we are are all offerings of gratitude, all responses to and expressions of the grace of Christ: FOR YOU KNOW THE GRACE OF OUR LORD JESUS CHRIST, THAT THOUGH HE WAS RICH, YET FOR YOUR SAKE HE BECAME POOR, SO THAT BY HIS POVERTY YOU MIGHT BECOME RICH.

And so that we, becoming rich, might ourselves in turn become poor for the sake of others. Don't you see this wonderful pattern of grace? God's people emptying themselves of their strengths, money, wisdom, power, goodness, and love (graces all!) that others may be filled.

18
Call to Battle
(10:1-6)

Something has happened between the end of 2 Corinthians 9 and the beginning of chapter 10. We cannot know for certain what has happened, but we sense that the conflict has escalated and that Paul is mounting a furious counterattack.

Up to this point Paul has been content to argue his points theologically with the Corinthians and to refer only indirectly to his opponents, as if to say, "If the glove fits, wear it." But beginning with this chapter Paul puts his own gloves on, boxing gloves. We hear a more urgent tone in his voice. Has Paul heard that the methods of the first nine chapters have failed in persuading the Corinthians away from the lures of the invading SUPER-APOSTLES? If so, then the last chapters of this letter, 10—13, represent another letter, an impassioned follow-up to 2 Corinthians 1—9.

Chapter 10:1-6 is a call to battle. Paul begins by appealing to them BY THE MEEKNESS AND GENTLENESS OF CHRIST. Then he refers to himself using the very words of accusation hurled at him: I WHO AM HUMBLE WHEN FACE TO FACE WITH YOU, BUT BOLD TO YOU WHEN I AM AWAY! (v. 1). His adversaries have made fun of him by saying that Paul barks louder the further he is away. Paul counters that he will be as humble or bold as the situation dictates, geography beside the point.

Paul is ready to fight, but he is careful to define the limits of the battle and the careful choice of weapons. His opponents accuse him of ACTING IN A WORLDLY FASHION (v. 2), literally "walking according to the flesh." (Have his opponents turned Paul's words against him?) Paul counters that though we live in the flesh we do not battle in the ways of the flesh, for our weapons of war are not worldly/fleshly but are spiritual. These weapons have DIVINE POWER TO DESTROY STRONGHOLDS, power which overthrows REASONINGS and every PROUD OBSTA-CLE TO THE KNOWLEDGE OF GOD.

The goal of the battle is TO TAKE EVERY THOUGHT CAP-TIVE TO OBEY CHRIST (v. 5). What a grand and expansive goal: to take every thought captive to the lordship of Christ. Such holy war, however, must be fought with holy armaments. Persua-sion not coercion is the way. In trying to defeat the enemy we must not adopt its violent weapons thus becoming the enemy. We do not fight *kata sarx,* according to the flesh, but *kata pneuma,* accord-ing to the spirit.

Now Paul begins a new round of self-defense. He hates doing this, but he must. As Beasley-Murray aptly suggests, he is like a motorist driving with his brakes on. Opponents have suggested in the presumption of their own supreme Christlikeness that Paul might not even belong to Christ. Paul answers: IF ANYONE IS CONFIDENT THAT HE IS CHRIST'S, LET HIM REMIND HIMSELF THAT AS HE IS CHRIST'S, SO ARE WE (v. 7).

Paul does not like having to boast in his authority. In fact, this is only the second time in all his letters that he uses this word *(exousia)* in connection with his apostolic authority. (The other is in 1 Cor. 9.) But now he must because his opponents have made apostolic authority, his versus theirs, the issue. Paul is careful to define the use of authority. It is the power God gives his apostles for BUILDING YOU UP AND NOT FOR DESTROYING YOU (v. 8). Power can be used for either building up or tearing down, but true apostolic authority, power from the Lord, is used only to build up.

Paul answers another charge—HIS LETTERS ARE WEIGHTY AND STRONG, BUT HIS BODILY PRESENCE IS WEAK, AND HIS SPEECH OF NO ACCOUNT (v. 10). This charge is obviously made by visiting apostles who glory in their personal appearance and eloquence. Paul answers with the stron-gest possible appeal to proper apostolic conduct, two rules for apostolic ethics. First, we should not build ourselves up by tearing others down. WHEN THEY COMPARE THEMSELVES WITH ONE ANOTHER, THEY ARE WITHOUT UNDERSTANDING (v. 12). Secondly, we should not go into churches established by others capitalizing on work formerly done and boast as if it is all our work. WE DO NOT BOAST BEYOND LIMIT, IN OTHER MEN'S LABORS (v. 15).

Paul's calling is to go all over the world starting churches. If he has any boast it is only in the ever-expanding mission to the Gentiles. What galls him is that other apostles should go into churches already established and boast of WORK ALREADY DONE IN ANOTHER'S FIELD (v. 16). Paul's priority was in starting churches. He is not denying the importance of the pastoral task which follows the evangelistic/church starting tasks, but he is saying that these pastor/apostles who come later should have the grace to honor and commend the work already established and the worker who established it. God forbid that they, as these opponents are in fact doing, should denigrate their predecessors and claim all good progress for their own.

Paul concludes this section with a quotation from Scripture: LET HIM WHO BOASTS, BOAST OF THE LORD (v. 17). False apostles are busy with self-praise, often at the expense of other apostles. True apostles are concerned only with the commendation of the Lord.

19
A Fool's Speech
(11:1 to 12:13)

Victor Paul Furnish has perceptively labeled this section, "a fool's speech."[1] Paul himself has framed it (11:1 and 12:11) as the talk of a fool. It is a carefully constructed speech designed to combat the boasting of the SUPER-APOSTLES. It is deeply ironic in form and character because while he boasts and boasts like a fool, he boasts not in his strength, as do his opponents, but in his weakness. This chapter will provide a guide through the entire length of the speech. The following two chapters will provide exposition of the key polemic of the letter, the false gospel of the super-apostles versus the true gospel of the suffering apostolate (ch. 20) and the key paradox of the letter: strength in weakness (ch. 21), which is the heart of the letter and the heart of Paul's gospel.

I

I WISH YOU WOULD BEAR WITH ME IN A LITTLE FOOLISHNESS (11:1). How embarrassing this is for Paul, but for the sake of the gospel he is willing to make himself a fool once again. I feel a DIVINE JEALOUSY FOR YOU (v. 2), he says. And he uses the betrothal/marriage customs of the time as a metaphor: I am like a father who has betrothed you my church, my daughter, to be married to Christ and pledging as any good father to keep you pure for your husband until you are married.

This is a remarkable image and is used with proper theological reserve. The apostle or pastor is not betrothed to the church as husband. The church says its marriage vows to Christ. The pastor/apostle is like a father who promises his daughter to Christ, or like a friend introducing her friend to Christ, or like the minister counseling a couple to be married and performing the wedding ceremony. The church is the bride of Christ, not of the pastor. Paul goes on: I promised you my daughter-church to Christ, but there have been deceitful ones who have come into the church to lead you ASTRAY FROM A SINCERE AND PURE DEVOTION TO CHRIST (v. 3).

Now he turns up the attack: These persons have come into your midst preaching ANOTHER JESUS, offering A DIFFERENT SPIRIT and presenting A DIFFERENT GOSPEL (v. 4). The invading apostles are preaching the false gospel of another Jesus.

Paul defends himself: I am not in the least bit inferior to these SUPERIOR-APOSTLES (v. 5). I may not be as skilled in public speaking, but I am not unskilled in KNOWLEDGE (v. 6). (One is reminded of the North Carolina senator, Sam Ervin, always prefacing his down-home eloquence with the sly disclaimer, "I'm just a country lawyer.")

Then Paul addresses what has become a surprisingly troubling issue.[2] What he had considered an act of love on his part has been turned against him. Because the combination of his tentmaking wages and the contributions from the much poorer congregation in Macedonia had SUPPLIED HIS NEEDS, Paul did not BURDEN the Corinthians by asking for financial support. In Paul's mind it is right that an apostle/pastor have basic needs met, but not right for that person to get rich on the church's generosity. Paul already had "enough" so he would not ask for more—a far cry from some present-day TV preachers who get rich from the offerings of the masses and call their wealth a "blessing," modern-day SUPER-APOSTLES.

The invading super-apostles had turned Paul's well-intentioned policy against him. They said that it was an honor for God's people to support an apostle and to refuse their support was an insult. These opponents in turn were most eager to receive support as if it in and of itself authenticated their apostleship. Moreover they may well have even implied that Paul's offering for the poor in Jerusalem was in fact—at least in part—a private slush fund from which Paul derived income for himself (See 12:16-17). Paul was innocent, but contemporary heirs of the SUPER-APOSTLES, media

evangelists, have learned this trick well, often benefitting themselves from offerings gains through tearful mission pleas.

Paul asks, DID I COMMIT A SIN by preaching GOD'S GOS-
PEL WITHOUT COST TO YOU? (v. 7). The invading apostles
have made it seem so. But Paul is resolute: I REFRAINED AND
WILL REFRAIN FROM BURDENING YOU (v. 9).

Now Paul escalates his attack another notch. These men disguise themselves as APOSTLES OF CHRIST but they are
FALSE APOSTLES, literally pseudoapostles. They claim to
work in God's vineyard but they are DECEITFUL WORKMEN
(v. 3). Even Satan clothes himself in light, and these men disguise
themselves as Christ's apostles.

To compete with them I will boast, Paul says, even if that makes
me a fool. FOR YOU GLADLY BEAR WITH FOOLS (v. 19),
Paul says. You bear it, how I do not know, when a man boasting of
his strength comes into your church and MAKES SLAVES OF
YOU and PREYS UPON YOU, and TAKES ADVANTAGE OF
YOU, and PUTS ON AIRS, and STRIKES YOU IN THE FACE
(v. 20). We, says Paul, were TOO WEAK (v. 21) to do that, and
now we are being called WEAKLINGS.

Well, now, if they want to brag I'll brag with them. Then he
begins verse 1 of "Anything You Can Do I Can Do Better!" I feel
like a fool singing this, but I'll go ahead:

> You call yourself HEBREWS?
>   SO AM I!
> You boast of being ISRAELITES?
>   I'M ONE, TOO!
> DESCENDANTS OF ABRAHAM?
>   SO AM I!
> SERVANTS OF CHRIST?
>   I'm a better one by far!

Now I'm really talking LIKE A MADMAN, Paul interrupts his
song to say. What is crazier than bragging over who's the greatest
servant! Well, if you want to brag about medals of service, here's
mine, from purple heart to congressional medal of honor. If you

want to brag with me, here's my list of commendations, not from
my victories but from my troubles:

imprisonments	in danger: in the city,
countless beatings	in the wilderness, and
often near death	from false brethren
five times the forty lashes	toil and hardship
three times beaten with rocks	sleepless nights
shipwrecked	in hunger and thirst
adrift at sea	in cold and exposure
frequent journeys	daily pressure of
in danger from: rivers,	anxiety for all
robbers, my own people,	my churches
Gentiles	

Who's not WEAK; We're all WEAK! Paul says. And I, an apostle, am WEAK along with you. And if anyone of you trip and fall
because of the false gospel being foisted on you, am I not right to
be INDIGNANT? (v. 29).

These are my medals, Paul exclaims, not the kind of medals
many people would brag about. IF I MUST BOAST [and this fine
mess we find ourselves in forces me to], I WILL BOAST IN MY
WEAKNESS (v. 30).

Paul goes on to talk about his escape from the Damascus prison
and he, for the first time, relates his highest spiritual experiences
(but modestly in the third person). But now he comes to the climax
of the speech and to the heart of his gospel. It was at the occasion
of my greatest weakness, MY THORN IN THE FLESH, a thorn
left there after so many long nights and unanswered prayers that I
received the greatest revelation of all: MY GRACE IS SUFFI-
CIENT FOR YOU; FOR MY STRENGTH IS MADE PERFECT
IN WEAKNESS (12:9).

From this extraordinary disclosure, Paul has been able to make
sense of his human experience and of his calling as an apostle of
Christ, a kind of sense revealed and hidden in the mystery of the
cross. With this understanding Paul is able to meet anything that
comes his way: FOR WHEN I AM WEAK, THEN I AM
STRONG (v. 10).

Paul closes with his final admission of folly. I HAVE BEEN A FOOL, this is a fool's speech you've been hearing, but the boasting of these PSEUDO-APOSTLES has forced me into it. The last sentence reveals the crazy contradiction of this fool's speech: FOR I WAS NOT AT ALL INFERIOR TO THESE SUPER-APOSTLES EVEN THOUGH I AM NOTHING (v. 11).

But it is a crazy contradiction which has become the wisdom of God for those who follow the Christ, the Christ who said finding comes in losing and who hung on the cross as the King of the world.

Notes

1. Furnish, pp. 485 *ff.*
2. Ibid., pp. 506-509 for a superb discussion of money issue.

20
The Battle Today:
The False Gospel
of Another Jesus

(11:1-21)

A South American film of the 1970s, *El Topo,* presented an unforgettable scene. The movie was a critique of Western society, and its setting was a town in the wild West. All over town the symbol was erected: a giant triangle with a human eye in the middle. Later I was to see the same symbol on the back of a dollar bill. No elaboration needed.

The people went into their church on Sunday morning and the symbol of the church was the same as the town's: a triangle with an eye. It loomed before the congregation behind the pulpit on a huge banner, floor to ceiling, where churches normally have their altars or baptistries.

The worship service went like this: the minister and his young assistant went to the front of the church. The pastor pulled a six-shooter from his robe, put one bullet in the chamber, spun the chamber, stuck the gun to his head, and pulled the trigger. *Click.* The people chanted their litany: "God will protect us, God will protect us." Then the gun was passed throughout the congregation. Other worshipers would spin the chamber, put the gun to their heads. *Click.* "God will protect us, God will protect us," they chanted. Then a woman handed the gun to the new young associate pastor. This was his first service. He looked at the gun, afraid to play the game of religious roulette. The pastor whispered in his ear so no one else could hear: "Don't be afraid—it's only a blank."

The idealistic young minister was shocked at the deception. Turning aside, he pulled the blank out and put a real bullet in,

spun the chamber, put it to his head and pulled the trigger. *Click.*
"God will protect us." Then unexpectedly a person grabbed the
gun and began to pass the gun through the congregation. *Click.*
"God will protect us. God will protect us." Then a young boy
took the gun, spun the chamber, and pulled the trigger. The gun
went off. The boy was dead. The people fled. Their religion lay
dead, as dead as the body of that young boy.

Later in the day, the young associate pastor returned to the
church, angry and disillusioned. He stood under the banner which
held the symbol and ripped it down. And behind it stood . . . the
cross.

I

Paul minces no words about these opponents he calls SUPER-
APOSTLES. They are FALSE APOSTLES who preach AN-
OTHER JESUS, A DIFFERENT SPIRIT, and a DIFFERENT
GOSPEL (11:4). Convinced that subtle theological teaching will
not defeat his opponents, Paul now becomes polemical and severe.
There comes a point where variations of the gospel become false
gospels. Paul discerns that his opponents have crossed that line.

Who were these men? Let me summarize from our study of the
text and from the contributions of historians who have given us a
glimpse of the religious atmosphere of that first-century Hellenistic world.

They were traveling missionaries probably of Hellenistic/
Jewish background—their predilection for ecstatic religious experience and "divine-man" theology place them comfortably in that
Hellenistic world. They were blue-blooded Jews converted to a
kind of Christianity that reflected their culture-religion more than
the historical Jesus of Nazareth. They gloried in their personal
strength, their great spiritual experiences, their obedience to the
Law, their eloquence, their handsome appearance and their success. They lorded it over the congregations they visited, tyrannizing their faith, milking them for money, and bragging on their
success. They lived unashamedly well off the offerings of these
congregations. In turn they sought to undermine Paul's apostle-

ship, scoffing at his weakness and lack of personal appearance and eloquence. They preached a religion of health, wealth and success—themselves Exhibit A.

It sold well in the religious marketplace of the first-century Hellenistic world, and it sells well today. But it is the false gospel of another Jesus.

II

The history of the church is filled with examples of those who preach the false gospel of another Jesus. They have covered up the cross with their own most highly valued symbols. These persons ignore the Jesus revealed in Scripture, the historical Jesus born into this world, crucified, and risen. Instead they have created ANOTHER JESUS in their own image.

Instead of seeing Jesus as he *is*, they see him *kata sarx,* FROM A HUMAN POINT OF VIEW (4:16), that is, they remake him in their own image. A Marxist writes a poem and calls him Comrade Jesus—as if Jesus was a Marxist revolutionary. An American businessman calls him "the greatest salesman who ever lived"—as if the gospel were something to be merchandised and the disciples were the beginning of the sales pyramid. If Jesus can mean anything to anybody, then who is he really? When we see Jesus *kata sarx,* we ignore the real Jesus and make him in our image. Our minds then mock the psalmist's praise, "This is the day which the Lord has made" (Ps. 118:24). This is the Lord the day has made! The false gospel of another Jesus.

III

The SUPER-APOSTLES had invaded Corinth preaching such a false gospel and it is not so different from the false gospel being preached with great success in America today. The super-apostles are with us today promoting a religion of super-pastors, super-Christians, and super-churches. Their pseudogospel has a false Christology, a false theology, a false spirituality, a false "clergyology," and a false ecclesiology. (Paul draws his distinctions in black and white polemical extremes. Sometimes, that is the only way we can see. The contrasts I draw here are similarly extreme.

Most churches and ministers live somewhere in between. For example, God calls us to minister our of weakness and out of strength; pastors can abdicate their authority, be properly authoritative, or be improperly authoritarian.)

The False Christology of a Super-Christ

The false gospel's Christology is Jesus as super-man. He is divinity devoid of humanity, supremely powerful, wise, righteous, and rich. Political cartoonist Doug Marlette once pictured Jesus in a ragged robe and received a hostile letter to the editor arguing that Jesus wore a "seamless robe," the robe of a wealthy man. How dare Marlette picture him poor!

This false Christology paints himself powerful as all earthly rulers, only more so. From this perspective, the way of the cross was an aberration from his otherwise successful life. It was necessary only to complete the transaction of our salvation. According to their formulas, any humiliation he suffered was for our exaltation: Christ became poor so we might become rich, he became human so we might become divine, he became weak so we might become strong, he suffered that we might escape suffering. This Jesus came to earth to lift us up out of this world's tribulation and to make us victors in this life. The images of Christ are exclusively regal and victorious. Such a Christ is always on the side of the powerful.

In contrast, Paul had met the Suffering Christ—the crucified Messiah and risen Lord—whose suffering was more than a brief transaction for salvation's sake but was the way of the son of God in a world of sin and tragedy. And it was also the model for ministry in his name: as we partake in Christ's sufferings we shall one day partake of his glory.

The False Theology: A Theology of Glory

The false gospel's theology is what Martin Luther called a "theology of glory."[1] It is a theology for the strong. Despite its protests to the contrary, it believes in self-salvation: by my own power or goodness or wits. It looks for God only in symbols of victory. James and John are its patron saints, hustling to sit by

Jesus' right and left hand in glory, unaware that the cup about to be drunk is the cup of suffering (Mark 10:35 *ff.*). To a theology of glory the cross is as much a stumbling block as it was to Greeks and as much a scandle as it was to Jews (1 Cor. 1:18 *ff.*). Little does it know that the cross is the power and wisdom of God.

A theology of glory trades in the power and success of its culture. It borrows the ascendent cultural symbols and with them covers up the cross. We may not crassly put dollar signs over the altar, but why do so many American churches built early in our century look like banks or courthouses, and why do so many contemporary worship centers look like performing arts centers?

This theology is a theology of health, wealth, and success. It says that if you're a Christian, you'll be blessed and lead a triumphant Christian life. If you love Jesus and have enough faith ("enough faith" is the one qualifier that gets the preacher/promiser off the hook), you'll enjoy health, wealth, and success.

This false gospel of another Jesus is paraded before our eyes on TV. Someone quipped that TV religion is to true religion what professional wrestling is to the real sport. The quip is hyperbole, but what is alarming is that what TV religion often offers is only a slightly exaggerated form of a culture-religion practiced in many churches today: the false gospel of another Jesus.

Worship services have become a pious form of entertainment. Applause has replaced the Amen corner. Guest stars are given spots to tell how Christ has given them success.

What this religion promises is unbelievable. Its favorite verse is 3 John 1:2: "I wish above all that you would prosper and be in health." It turns that simple blessing into a blank check that God gives us to endorse anytime we want to—as long as we ask "believing." We are told to "put in our orders" to God, to ask for everything from houses to diamond rings, to healing, to promotions. That method works best for TV preachers who make their requests known not only to God but also before millions of viewers—and it is we viewers who most often end up answering their prayers.

This is the false gospel of another Jesus. *There are some things that Jesus just did not promise.* God wants the best and works for the best for all his children, but Jesus did not promise us fancy houses or diamond rings. He talked more about giving up things like that than getting them. A theology of glory is the perfect religion for a nation bent on military superiority, fascinated with game shows and lotteries and get-rich-quick schemes. It is quite different from the religion of Jesus.

In contrast, Paul answers with a theology of the cross. The cross is the way of God's love in history, a suffering love which is redeeming the world but which will not be a triumphant love until the kingdom in fullness comes. Its favorite verse is Romans 8:28: "For we know that in everything God works for good [not *goods*] with those who love him, who are called according to his purpose." God does not promise us the unblemished best of times but that in everything, the good and the bad, God is working His good purpose out.

The gospel of the real Jesus does not abolish suffering or rescue us from suffering; rather it teaches us how to bear suffering and sends us into the suffering world with the balms of God.

False Spirituality: Summertime All the Time

The false gospel's spirituality is exclusively "summery," for the church is an elite club for super-Christians. Martin Marty following Karl Rahner has identified two kinds of spirituality, a summery kind and a wintry kind.[2] There are, to be sure, different seasons of the heart. Sometimes we walk through the summertime of the heart, other times we trudge through winter. Depression, divorce, bankruptcy, death have cast us into winter. Other people have a wintertime cast to their personalities; and their melancholy is not of their choosing but is their natural season.

There are spiritualities which correspond to these seasons. Summery spirituality lives in the warm immediacy of God's presence. The Holy Spirit fills your heart, Jesus feels close, all's well and you sing "Victory in Jesus" or "There Is Sunshine In My Soul Today."

A wintry spirituality helps a person struggling through winter.

It WALKS BY FAITH NOT BY SIGHT (2 Cor. 5:7). It experiences God's absence more than his presence and walks like *Hebrews'* faith pilgrims who "died in faith, not having received what was promised, but having seen it and greeted it from afar" (Heb. 11:13). A wintry sort of spirituality "hangs in there" when God seems so far away and worship feels meaningless and Scriptures read like a foreign language.

Some people have a more wintry personality, not necessarily sadder but more analytical, more apt to be observers of life. Living a step back they take a longer look and become astute observers of patterns. A wintry sort of spirituality will fit their temperament and help them offer their own unique gifts to the church.

Both wintry and summery spiritualities have their own integrity. God is a God "for all seasons." The false spirituality of the false gospel is a twelve-month-of-the-year exclusively summery spirituality. Popular religion in America is all summer. Most TV religion is July Fourth every Sunday! Summery spirituality is all smiles. It chooses only happy hymns (most of the lament-like hymns have been taken out of our hymn books); it reads only summery psalms and ignores the abundance of wintry psalms (the psalms are songs for all seasons of the heart). It voices only the victories of the Christian life.

What this kind of worship and spirituality does is to make outsiders of wintry sorts of people or people walking through winter. These people feel like they are out in the snow looking in the window at people sitting around a warm hearth. They wonder, *Why am I in the cold out here and they are in there?*

Summery spirituality also ignores those persons whose plight in life places them at the margins of society. It is a gospel for the well-heeled. (It is apt to say to the poor "Go in peace, be warmed and filled," without giving them anything for the body—Jas. 2:16). It does not want to listen to people's hurt and pain or encounter any hint of winter.

But this is the false gospel of another Jesus. Jesus walks with us in all seasons. God is as much a God of winter as summer and is faithful in all seasons. "Great Is Thy Faithfulness," we sing, and as we walk with such a God both our summer and winter will praise him.

False "Clergyology": The Super-Pastor

The false gospel has its own theology of clergy: the super-pastors. The super-apostles have trained them well. The super-apostles had an excessively authoritarian style of leadership—they "lord[ed] it over" the congregation's faith and life (1:24). They bragged about their spiritual superiority (12:1), traded in earthly commendations (3:1), and, in Paul's words, made slaves of the people, preyed upon them, took advantage of them and put on airs (11:20).

Today super-pastors are their successors. Found in churches of varying sizes and theological persuasion, they glory in their personal strengths, their handsome camera-ready looks, their studied eloquence, their health, wealth, and success. They often live better than their flock. And why not, remarked one TV evangelist, "God wants his ministers to go first class." And aren't riches a sign of God's blessing on our ministry?

The super-pastor is authoritarian in leadership-style. The pastor is male because, according to their interpretation of Scripture, women cannot hold authority over men (1 Cor. 11:2-16; 14:34-36; 1 Tim. 2:11-15). He is "ruler" of the church. He is the final interpreter of Scripture for the congregation. He is the C.E.O. unilaterally making the major decisions of the corporation called church.

The super-pastor trades in the currency of the culture-god of success: if it is successful it must be right. The numerical growth of the church proves its faithfulness. The pastor's success holds out hope for the laity that *they* can be a success too. Mass media is the great image-maker which props up this religion, giving the veneer of success to every one who is on the air. The constant appeals for money on the air-waves ensure the purchase of more air-time which makes the pastor look successful . . . and on and on.

The super-pastor images himself in the power/wealth mode of society. He dresses for success. In contrast Paul speaks of being YOUR SERVANTS FOR CHRIST'S SAKE. Inasmuch as they lead, true apostles and pastors lead as servants. They dress for service. (See chap. 9.) This is the kind of pastoral leadership the church needs, leadership that cares for the flock of God patiently and tenderly, as a servant-shepherd.

False Ecclesiology: Super-Church

The false gospel has its own theology of the church: the super-church.[3] It is the logical and inevitable conclusion to its train of false theologies.

The super-church may be big, but bigness is not its necessary definition. A church can be big without being a super-church, and a church may not be big but have a super-church attitude. Super-church has more to do with *character* than with size. Super-church is a mentality of ministry, a self-image which shapes its mission. Super-church in America has (at least) these seven marks of identification (see also the Overture).

1. It locates itself in the pleasure-zones of society. Every community has its pleasure zones and pain zones: pleasure zones like suburbs and shopping malls, pain zones like slums and hospitals and prisons. Frequently the super-church vacates pain zones and moves from slums and inner cities to the suburbs. Its location may stay in a pain zones of the city, but its immediate surrounding is not its focus of ministry. It sits in sublime oblivion to the pain around it. People who drive in to the church would rarely go to anything else in the pain zone. The super-church hides its face from the wounded ones and wounded places, just as people hid their faces from Isaiah's Suffering Servant.

2. Bigger is better is blessed. The criterion for authenticity is growth. Huge worship centers are built to accommodate large crowds and are designed as performance halls for the new kind of worship. They are camera-ready for sound and light. The focus is on the stage, not the congregation. One pastor was heard to say that he had limited the size of his new worship center to six thou-

sand seats because when you get over six thousand people to-gether you lose the personal touch. And he wasn't joking.

3. A preoccupation with psychological and private moral con-cerns and an avoidance of larger social issues. It manifests the "triumph of the therapeutic" and the triumph of moralism. God's broader concerns for the health of society and the righteousness of the nation is ignored. (There is a range of moral concerns ad-dressed, but these are typically individual moral concerns, there-fore, only part of the gospel is being preached.) A prominent, West-Coast pastor advised pastors never to preach on social is-sues. That will kill church growth, he said.

4. Its worship is all triumphant. No sad hymns, no classical music, and no songs, advised one church growth expert, in a mi-nor key! Only victories can be voiced. Worship is happy time—but far from the joy Paul experienced in his imprisonment and adversity. Woundedness is rarely mentioned in such worship, and wounded people do not generally feel welcome at the summery worship of the super-church.

5. Super-church has such an abundance of personal and finan-cial resources that instead of carrying on its work *through* a de-nomination it often seeks to do the work *of* a denomination.[4] It runs its own schools and sends its own missionaries. It starts clonelike churches in other places. Most of its money stays inside its own budget because it is trying to do the work of a denomina-tion. There is a pride of singularity—we alone are preaching the gospel—and it finds whole-hearted involvement in its own denom-ination or ecumenical fellowship with other denominations diffi-cult.

6. Membership is consumer oriented rather than mission ori-ented. Someone has called it *McChurch!* Membership has less to do with getting vitally and personally involved in some mission or ministry and more to do with attending, giving an offering, and enjoying services rendered, religious consumer goods. Huge churches are constructed on that model—to render services. They are not built to get people involved in mission.

7. Its politics—spoken and unspoken, visible and invisible but

always there—is most often the politics of the powerful. It favors the haves over the have-nots. It enjoys worship with people in positions of power, and it advocates policies that can become a politics of selfishness. In America, as someone has quipped, the poor are getting poorer and the rich are getting religious!—and where they (the richer) go to church is super-church. The poor and powerless, the weak and outcast, people of color and people in pain go someplace else.

In contrast, Paul speaks of a servant-church, a church willing to identify with the poor and with those on the margins of society. It is willing to follow Christ to the "least of these." It is willing to give to its fullness—its wealth, power, talent and wisdom—for the sake of the empty, willing to SPEND and BE SPENT for their sake. It is willing to look more modest so that it may serve more generously. It is willing to be a prophet-church, taking on the power structures which ignore the powerless and calling them to rule with justice and mercy. It is willing to face all that life brings—wealth and poverty, victories and defeats—in the Spirit of Christ who is its only sufficiency.

The church of the false gospel of another Jesus is widely acclaimed, but we should not despair. By the grace of God the real Christ makes himself known even within versions of Christianity that are perversions of his face. We *all* pervert the gospel to some degree, and God graciously stays with us, seeking to renovate our hearts and reform our mission. The Spirit of the true Christ is at work among us, even now. The Reformation had the great slogan: "The church reformed but always to be reformed."[5] We are a church in cultural captivity awaiting a New Reformation.

It may begin with some disillusioned young disciple who goes to the banner hanging over the altar—the one with the triangle and eye—and pulls it down and discovers behind it . . . the cross.

Notes

1. See also Overture for treatment of theology of glory vs. theology of the cross.

2. Martin Marty, *A Cry of Absence: Reflections for the Winter of the Heart* (New York: Harper & Row, 1983).

3. See also Overture for treatment of super-church vs. servant-church.

4. This distinction was made to me by William R. O'Brien, executive vice president for the Foreign Mission Board of the Southern Baptist Convention.

5. Robert McAfee Brown, *The Spirit of Protestantism* (New York: Oxford University Press, 1961), p. 44.

21

The Heart of the Paul's Gospel: Grace Sufficient, Strength in Weakness

(12:1-9)

Strong, upstanding, confident people may wriggle and squirm all they like; but there it is. Paul squirmed, too. Something he called a thorn stood there in the very sinews of his apostleship, humiliating him, insinuating its ugly self against all his plans, canceling his hopes one by one, or so it seemed to him, and it wouldn't budge. He tried to wriggle out into some measure of self-reliance three times by way of his prayer. He wanted a little bit of human wholeness under his feet to be a man on! "In God's name," he cried, "let me be free to run, free from this hounding infirmity that holds its nose at my heels!" And all he got on his lonely island of discontent was the hint and murmur of the sea, God's greatness around his incompleteness, round his restlessness God's rest! "It is enough that you have my grace." The word kept whispering itself down through the silence out of heaven; and it didn't seen right! He had preached to others about the weakness that was stronger than strength, and the foolish things that had been chosen to confound the wise; but it wasn't so easy to get hold of, now that his old winged sermon had come home to roost! It was like falling through endless space, getting such an answer as that, there in his closet, behind the closed door! Until the day he struck bottom! You've come up with it now; you've come up with the text! He knelt there, dazed suddenly at the distance he had fallen from his own esteem. But when he struggled up from his knees, it was GOD he had under his feet to be a man on! "My strength is made perfect in weakness."[1]

Those are Paul Scherer's words, and they form a stunning setting for what is at the heart of Paul's gospel: a grace sufficient and God's strength made perfect in weakness.

I

Those words *strength in weakness* are curious words, paradoxical words, but they strike at the heart of things, at the heart of reality and at the heart of Paul's gospel. Those words were not spoken by God into a vacuum. They were spoken into two critical circumstances of Paul's life: into a humiliating weakness Paul suffered and into the theological battle with the super-apostles. The two were not unconnected. To the super-apostles, Paul's weakness was obvious proof he was not a true apostle; for Paul, his weakness was one more occasion for the astonishing truth of the gospel to be made manifest. What was at stake was no less than the authenticity of Paul's apostleship, the shape of the gospel and the nature of the church's apostolic ministry. And the issues kept circling those two words: *strength* and *weakness*.

We've seen many striking contrasts in 2 Corinthians: super-apostles versus the suffering apostolate, a theology of glory versus a theology of the cross. Just as there are two kinds of apostles and two kinds of theology, there are also two kinds of ministry. The kind of ministry that goes with super-apostles and their theology of glory is *ministry through strength*. That strength may be in varying forms: wisdom, eloquence, wealth, spiritual experiences, power, and goodness.

In contrast, the kind of ministry that goes with the suffering apostolate and its theology of the cross is *ministry through weakness*. It is the way of the "wounded healer." In his book *The Wounded Healer* Henri Nouwen has come up with one of the most captivating images of ministry in recent years.[2] But it is an image as ancient as the servant songs of Isaiah which pictured God's servant as one acquainted with grief, an eyesore from whom we hid our faces, but one who bore the woundedness of the world and by whose stripes we find our healing. It is as ancient as God's Christ, who all lifelong identified with the wounded and who himself died a degrading death on a criminal's cross. It is as ancient as the apostle Paul who limped and wheezed across the Mediterranean world with a gospel that made him its fool.

Nouwen's image comes from the Jewish Talmud where the

Messiah is shockingly found sitting among the wounded and is himself wounded. He takes care of his bandages one at a time so he can be ready to minister to other's needs.

The issue is what does God's Messiah and the gospel of Christ have to do with human woundedness, and what kind of ministers does Christ call? False apostles preach a theology of glory which struts its strength and grins its way past life's shipwrecks. In contrast, the true gospel of Jesus Christ preaches a theology of the cross. True apostles share in the sufferings of Christ as they honestly bear their own suffering and as they enter into the suffering of others. The capacity to enter into the sufferings of others depends upon our capacity to face our own weakness, and our capacity to face our own weakness has to do with yielding it to the mercy and power of God.

True ministry has to do with more than the use of our strength—the way of super-apostles—it also involves the consecrated offering of our weaknesses to God as we, the suffering apostolate, become wounded healers.

II

Paul has been defending the nature of true apostolic ministry. Chapter 12 carries on the defense. He begins this chapter by pretending to get into a bragging contest with the "spiritual giants" he calls super-apostles. If you want to brag about spiritual experiences, I'll brag too. It is verse 2 of "Anything You Can Do I Can Do Better!" (V. 1 is in ch. 11.)

He shares his own spectacular spiritual encounters, but out of modesty speaks of himself in the third person:

"I know a man in Christ who fourteen years ago was snatched up into the highest heaven, even to the gates of Paradise. He heard wonderful things, things so wonderful they could not be put into words. I could boast all day about this man but I will not. Of myself I will only boast of my weakness" (12:1-6, author's paraphrase).

Paul was speaking the truth here. How many times have you heard Paul mention these great spiritual experiences? This is the only time. The super-apostles built their whole authority on experiences like these. Paul refused to speak of them.

Then Paul unwraps his wound. He said, I have been given A THORN IN THE FLESH (v. 7). Without it I might be like you super-apostles, puffed up and giddy with success! A THORN IN THE FLESH I HAVE. The image Paul used is more terrible than its translation suggests. Not a small thorn: *a giant stake.* Not mildly irritated, Paul was *impaled* by an affliction at times too great to bear.

We don't know what this thorn in the flesh was. The history of its exegesis reads like a medical textbook: everything from foot disease to eye disease, from epilepsy to obsessions to manic depressive illness. Whatever it was, it was not a private, mild irritation. It was public, agonizing, and humiliating affliction. It was a thorn lodged "in the very sinews of his apostleship" because it hindered his plans and became an issue with his adversaries: if he is so afflicted, how can he be an apostle?

It was a constant torment for he, as we all, "wanted a little bit of human wholeness under his feet to be a man on!"

III

And then one of the bravest verses of all the Bible. Paul says, "three times I asked to be delivered, three times I asked the Lord to take away that thorn." Three times he prayed but his plea was not answered (12:8, author's paraphrase).

Out of the silence of heaven came an answer, not the answer Paul wanted, but all the answer he needed. Paul, "my grace is sufficient for thee." My grace is enough. The first hint of that answer must have been difficult to hear. "Lord, that is not what I asked for. I asked to be free from this hounding infirmity." But as the answer came and came again he discovered that it was enough, this grace. Paul hit bottom with this thorn and all those unanswered prayers. But as Paul Scherer said in his matchless prose, "when he struggled up from his knees, it was God he had under his feet to be a man on."

"My strength is made perfect in weakness" (v. 9, KJV).

IV

This answer of God to Paul was not just a word of grace-full assurance; it was also a word of holy calling. God said, I will give you grace to carry on. You will make it. MY GRACE IS SUFFICIENT. That was the grace-full assurance. But God also gave him the most profound glimpse of the nature of his calling to be a minister of Christ Jesus: MY STRENGTH IS MADE PER-FECT IN WEAKNESS. That's it. WE HAVE THIS TREASURE IN EARTHEN VESSELS so that the transcendent power of God can show through (4:7). God has chosen the foolish things of this world to confound the wise, the weak things to confound the pow-erful (1 Cor. 1:27).

MY STRENGTH IS MADE PERFECT IN WEAKNESS.

God's grace is sufficient for us. It will carry us through. But there is more. Our woundedness is part of our calling. Each of us is a wounded healer.

Thorton Wilder said it so well in his play on the Pool of Be-thesda. A disabled physician was waiting with all the other wounded ones by the pool, waiting for God's angel to come stir the waters so that they could jump in and be healed. The angel came and stirred the waters but as the doctor was about to plunge in, the angel stopped him: "Draw back, physician, this moment is not for you. . . . Without your wound where would your power be? It is your very remorse that makes your low voice tremble in the hearts of men. The very angels themselves cannot persuade the wretched and blundering children on earth as can one human being broken on the wheels of living. In Love's service only the wounded soldiers can serve."[3]

The wounded healer—this is the image of our common minis-try. Super-apostles pretending to be as angels cannot touch or be touched by the world's pain. Christian ministry hears its call when grace comes amid the hounding, humiliating infirmities of life: MY GRACE IS ENOUGH FOR YOU; FOR MY STRENGTH IS MADE PERFECT IN WEAKNESS.

You may feel that your wounds disqualify you from Christian service. No, to the contrary, they provide you an opportunity to walk beside the Suffering Messiah and to be, by his grace, a wounded healer.

Max Cleland, the head of the Veterans Administration under Jimmy Carter and a triple amputee from the Vietnam War, discovered this truth. I heard him at the end of a speech quote an old poem attributed to an injured Civil War soldier:

> I asked God for strength that I might achieve;
> I was made weak that I might learn humbly to obey.
> I asked for help that I might do greater things;
> I was given infirmity that I might do better things.
> I asked for riches that I might be happy;
> I was given poverty that I might be wise.
> I asked for power that I might have the praise of men;
> I was given weakness that I might feel the need of God.
> I asked for all things that I might enjoy life;
> I was given life that I might enjoy all things.
> I got nothing that I asked for, but everything I hoped for.
> Almost despite myself my unspoken prayers were answered.
> I among all men am most richly blessed.

And Cleland, sitting in a wheelchair, became an apostle like Paul.

Harry Emerson Fosdick, among the greatest preachers of our century, found a crushing depression, mental breakdown, and trip to a sanitarium the avenue to a deepened ministry and the pathway to the writing of one of the great books on prayer written in our time, *The Meaning of Prayer*. He said of that experience: "I learned to pray, not because I had adequately argued out prayer's rationality, but because I desperately needed help from a greater power than my own. I learned that God, much more than a theological proposition, is an immediately available resource."[4]

MY GRACE IS SUFFICIENT FOR MY STRENGTH IS PERFECT IN WEAKNESS.

George W. Truett, perhaps the greatest Southern Baptist preacher of our century, went through the agony of shooting his best friend and killing him in a hunting accident. From that time on people say his voice changed. It took on the depth of great pathos. And it moved people to Christ, the Wounded Healer.

Even those wounded by sin can be used by God's grace in ministry. Godric, Frederick Buechner's twelfth-century sinner turned saint, had a dream where John the Baptist was calling him:

> Burn! Burn! Serve man and God as fire does by driving back the night. Let thy very rage against thy sin burst into flame. Dwell here alone and by hot striving to be pure become a torch to light men's way and scorch the wings of fiends. Seek not saints to ease thy spirit's pain that thou mayst serve better. *Thy pain's itself thy service.* Godric, Burn for God![5]

The sick pain of guilt can be forgiven and your sin-scars made a pathway of ministry.

V

Some verses are illumined by study, some by prayer, others by persons' lives. This verse over and over again has been illumined by wounded persons who, in their very woundedness, have become ministers of grace, people who now give what they have received. GRACE SUFFICIENT.

Christ does not call us to be super-apostles oblivious to our own wounds and blind to the wounds of others. He calls us to be wounded healers. It is not a call to go around looking for suffering, as if the more we suffer the more righteous we are. Neither is it a call to parade our suffering before others as exhibitionists for Jesus' sake. It is a call to get in touch with our own woundedness so that we might share more deeply in the woundedness of the world. It is a call to go to those who weep over "broken things too broke to mend"[6] and offer them the healing balms of God. If we are willing to admit our weakness, perhaps we will let ourselves close enough to wounded people that Christ's grace might pour from our broken heart to theirs.

Our wounds do not disqualify us from Christ's service, neither do they in and of themselves qualify us. Rather as we bear them in the grace of Christ, they become vessels of grace. They are the opportunity to hear and to bear and to pass along God's answer to Paul in his humiliating weakness: MY GRACE IS SUFFICIENT FOR YOU; FOR MY STRENGTH IS MADE PERFECT IN WEAKNESS.

Yes, God wants to use our strengths, too, but if God depended on our strength alone, he would have precious little raw material to work with. By his grace he works with our weakness too! Isn't that how God works with us all, not just Paul and Luther and Fosdick and Truett, us too! It was Luther who came up with most of these paradoxical images of grace: God writes straight with a crooked stick, God rides the lame horse, God carves the rotten wood. And glory! Grace is enough.

Paul limped and wheezed his way around the Mediterranean world, a thorn lodged in the sinews of his apostleship, humiliating him, accusing him—you're no minister!—drawing the derision of the super-apostles, causing him to be a laughingstock, Christ's fool.

All he heard was an answer given after long nights of unanswered prayer: MY GRACE IS SUFFICIENT FOR YOU; FOR MY STRENGTH IS MADE PERFECT IN WEAKNESS. And it was. And it is.

Notes

1. Paul Scherer, *Facts that Undergird Life* (New York: Harper & Row, 1938), p. 142.

2. Henri Nouwen, *The Wounded Healer: Ministry in Contemporary Society* (New York: Doubleday & Co., 1972).

3. Thorton Wilder, *The Angel That Troubled the Waters* (New York: Coward McCann, 1928), p. 145.

4. Harry Emerson Fosdick, *The Living of These Days* (New York: Harper & Row, 1956), p. 75.

5. Frederick Buechner, *Godric* (San Francisco: Harper & Row, 1983), p. 143. Emphasis mine.

6. John Masefield's phrase cited by Hal Warlick, "Despair: A Human No" in *The Miracle of Easter* (Waco: Word Books, 1980), p. 29.

22
Vocation and Limitation
(12:1-10)

When you're young you think God uses your strengths. The older you get the more you realize he uses your weakness. Consider Simon Peter for a moment. On the day of Pentecost—surely in his prime—he preached and three thousand were converted. Some sermon, huh. But was that a greater witness than the day years later when Peter was crucified? Upside down, he requested, for he didn't think himself worthy to be crucified as his Lord had been, right side up. Remember Jesus' words to Peter by the seashore the day he recommissioned him?

> When you were young, you girded yourself and walked where you would; but when you are old, you will stretch out your hands, and another will gird you and carry you where you do not wish to go (John 21:18).

Indeed.

The truth of the gospel is that your calling as a disciple of Jesus Christ has as much to do with your weakness as your strength. Maybe more. Flannery O'Connor put it this way: "Vocation implies limitation," her own life as a writer who suffered the crippling illness and early death of lupus a remarkable witness to that truth. And such was the truth Paul heard when he heard God say to him in his weakness, MY GRACE IS SUFFICIENT FOR YOU, FOR MY STRENGTH IS MADE PERFECT IN WEAKNESS.

I

One dimension of this truth is what Ralph Waldo Emerson called "compensation" in his famous essay by that name.[1] If it is a truth of the physical world, a strong right eye compensating for a weak left eye, it is just as true for the spiritual world. Emerson begins by saying,

> Ever since I was a boy, I have wished to write a discourse on Compensation; for it seemed to me when very young, that on this subject life was ahead of theology, and the people knew more than the preachers taught.[2]

One of those compensations has to do with this: "strength grows out of weakness." The good, he says, are "befriended by weakness and defect." "As no man had ever a point of pride that was not injurious to him, so no man ever had a defect that was not somewhere made useful to him."[3] In a famous fable, a stag admired his horns and disliked his feet, but when the hunter came, his feet saved him, but afterward, caught in a thicket, his horns destroyed him. Therefore every man (and woman) "in his lifetime needs to thank his faults," because as he confronts his weakness "like the wounded oyster, he mends his shell with pearl." A person goes to sleep in good times, but,

> When he is punished, tormented, defeated, he has a chance to learn something; he has been put on his wits, on his manhood; he has gained facts; learns his ignorance, is cured of the insanity of conceit; has got moderation and real skill.[4]

This "compensation" may not be as automatic a law as Emerson would sometimes make it sound, but surely it is a gift of grace offered to all who undergo difficulty in life. Strength does grow from weakness. And as Emerson observed, life may be ahead of theology and common folk ahead of the preachers in the recognition of this truth.

At some point it was a surprise to Paul, who before conversion to Christ was himself a super-apostle of the Jews. But when he learned the truth, it changed everything for him. STRENGTH IN WEAKNESS was gospel to him and helped him live life in this earthly mix of pleasure and pain, triumph and tragedy, limitation and grace.

II

A person's life that especially illumines this passage of Scripture for us is that of the great Southern novelist, Flannery O'Connor. She was a brilliant young writer who had "escaped" home in Milledgeville, Georgia to pursue her literary career in the exalted circles of New York City. She had *made* it. She planned to write as a Southern novelist from outside the South. She thought she needed the distance, and she reveled in the stimulating company of the literary elite who surrounded her.

Then in 1951, when twenty-six years of age, she discovered she had lupus, the disease which had killed her father. She had to face the specter of debilitating pain, loss of mobility, and early death. But even more troubling was what else she had to face: the loss of her independence; she would have to move back home into her mother's house in Milledgeville, Georgia, where her mother could take care of her.

At first she greeted the news of her disease and all that went with it as a spiritual and vocational death sentence. She wrote in a letter:

> This is a Return I have faced and when I faced it I was roped and tied and resigned the way it is necessary to be resigned to death, and largely because I thought it would be the end of any creation, any writing, any WORK from me.[5]

But, in fact, the reverse happened. The terrible, imposed limitation became the prism through which her best works passed. She lived at home for fourteen years, battling her illness and writing some of the best fiction, and most profoundly theological fiction, of our day. She admitted later: "the best of my writing has been done here."

I am sure her calling, her WORK, was enhanced by her limitation. She slowed down and began to observe people more closely and reflect more carefully. But more, in her sickness she experienced what she once called "the shock of grace," the unexplainable miracle that "the good intrudes upon the evil." She wrote about opening our lives to this grace: "The force of habit and the weight of possessions close it (our lives) up again. You accept grace the quickest when you have the least."[6] She once said that "the Georgia writer's true country is not Georgia but Georgia is an entrance to it for him." She could just as easily have said, My true country is not my disease, but my disease is an entrance to my true country.

Her disease was not easy. She did not romanticize her affliction. In one letter she said she was "afflicted with time," an affliction many a homebound person suffers. Another letter had this poignant postscript: "P.S. Prayer's requested. I am sick of being sick."[7] Neither did she spiritualize her affliction. She would not let people sweetly suggest that her suffering drew her closer to Christ. Suffering can be a shared experience with Christ, she conceded, but so should every experience that is not sinful.[8] Through it all she kept an amazing good humor about her affliction. When she learned she would be on crutches the rest of her life she wrote a friend: "I will henceforth be a structure with flying buttresses."[9] She closed one letter, "cheers and screams."

Through it all, by gift of grace, her sickness became a "crucible of redemption," the terrible forge upon which her best WORK was fashioned. She wrote:

> I have never been anywhere but sick. In a sense sickness is a place, more instructive than a long trip to Europe, and it's always a place where there's no company, where nobody can follow. Sickness before death is a very appropriate thing and I think those who don't have it miss one of God's mercies.[10]

Sounds a bit strange, doesn't it? At one point Paul would have thought it strange, too, as he kept praying for that thorn to be removed, till he heard God saying: MY GRACE IS SUFFICIENT FOR YOU; FOR MY STRENGTH IS MADE PERFECT IN WEAKNESS.

Conclusion

I don't know where you fit in all this. I know that for most of us life hasn't turned out like we once thought or hoped it would. Ugly limitations have reared their heads. We have been met by the hard reality of life's limits—both from within and without—and we have found the world to be too strong for us: in the form of disease or failure or weakness that hounds our heels and trips us up.

The word of the gospel today is that limitation becomes the occasion of calling, not its repudiation. All vocation means going one way instead of another, choosing one path rather than another. It means limiting your options so you can pursue one goal with your best energies. It means *not* doing some things. Sometimes you make the choice; other times life makes the choice for you.

But in every case your weakness, your limitation, can be turned into vocation. I know a homebound woman who uses her solitude to pray and pray and pray. If we stopped praying on this earth it would crumble in the night. I know a man suffering schizophrenia who pioneered ministry to the mentally ill. I know a person who cannot preach like Peter or pray like Paul but who visits lonely people virtually every day and brings Christ to them.

One of America's great writers, Reynolds Price, recently survived a battle with cancer of the spine but lost the use of his legs and is now a paraplegic. But in the "rescued time" which has been his gift since then and in the limitations of his body and lifestyle, he has experienced the most productive period of his career.

One more example, this one from the field of science. Stephen W. Hawking is the world's greatest theoretical physicist; he is the Lucasian professor of mathematics at Cambridge University, the chair Sir Isaac Newton once filled. He is widely known as the smartest man in physics since Einstein. His latest work, *A Brief History of Time: From the Big Bang to Black Holes,* is a phenomenon, a physics book which is a best-seller. What is even more amazing is that he has Lou Gehrig's disease and can now move only one thumb. He gets around in a motorized wheelchair and talks and writes through a portable computer he has designed. He can only speak through the computer and can only write ten words a minute, but he has made some of the greatest contributions of science since Einstein and is on his way to making the next great contribution to science in our generation. "Science is a very good area for disabled people because it is mainly the mind," he says.[11] Vocation and limitation.

I could go on and on. But this sampling is enough for now, and I pray some consolation and hope for you. The good news of Jesus Christ is that God uses us in our limitations, that his grace is sufficient, that his strength is—can we believe it?—made perfect in weakness.

Notes

1. Ralph Waldo Emerson, "Compensation" in *Essays and English Traits*, The Harvard Classics, ed. Charles W. Eliot (New York: P. F. Collier, 1937), pp. 85 *ff.*)

2. Ibid., p. 85.

3. Ibid., pp. 97-98.

4. Ibid., p. 98.

5. Flannery O'Connor, *The Habit of Being,* ed. Sally Fitzgerald (New York: Farrar, Straus, Giroux, 1979), p. 224. I am also indebted to Ralph C. Wood's article "Talent Increased and Returned to God: The Spiritual Legacy of Flannery O'Connor's Letters," *Anglican Theological Review,* vol. 62, no. 2, pp. 153-167.

6. Ibid., p. 241.

7. Ibid., p. 581.

8. Ibid., p. 527.

9. Ibid., p. 251.

10. Ibid., p. 163.

11. See Richard C. Morais, "Genius Unbound" in *Forbes,* March 23, 1987, p. 142; and the review of *A Brief History of Time: From the Big Bang to Black Holes* by Raymond Sokolov, "Putting God Back in the Sky," *Wall Street Journal,* May 10, 1988; also the cover article for *Newsweek,* June 12, 1988, "Reading God's Mind," pp. 56 *ff.*

23
The Magnificent Defeat and the Sacrament of Failure
(12:14 to 13:10)

Paul is readying himself for another visit; for the THIRD TIME he will come. His servant-heart says: I WILL GLADLY SPEND AND BE SPENT FOR YOUR SOULS (12:15). Moreover he has heard all the charges against him—from deceit to taking advantage of them—and he is filled with fear! I FEAR THAT PERHAPS I MAY COME AND FIND YOU NOT WHAT I WISH, AND THAT YOU MAY FIND ME NOT WHAT YOU WISH. Paul fears that he will find the church still consumed in QUARRELING, JEALOUSY, ANGER, SELFISHNESS, SLANDER, GOSSIP, CONCEIT, AND DISORDER (v. 20). The church was hardly the kingdom of God on earth. And he fears that the church may have fallen out of love with him for all his weaknesses. What pastors do not live with that fear that a day will come when they are not what the church wants or when the church is no longer what they want. Moreover, I FEAR, says Paul, the unrepented sins will cause me to MOURN, to BEWAIL, even more.

This chapter deals with the prospects of failure in ministry and probes the mystery of success and failure hid in the cross. I shall make use of two major images: the "Magnificent Defeat" disclosed in the mystery of Holy Week; and the "Sacrament of Failure," John Oman's description of the "forgotten sacrament"—the shaking off of the dust.

In this precarious world of sin and evil held in the providence of God and being redeemed by the peculiar onslaught of grace, God's ministers are always faced with the issue of success and failure. Therefore, we need the wisdom of the cross which teaches us how to succeed and how to fail.

I

Sometimes we succeed and sometimes we fail. Sometimes when we succeed we are failing and sometimes when we fail we are in fact succeeding. There are those times when failure is just failure and apparent success is real success, but Jesus, especially in that week called Holy Week teaches us to look beneath the surface and to seek the deeper victories of God.

Sometimes we succeed, sometimes we fail, but true success and failure is hid in the mystery of the cross, in the weakness of the cross that has become the power of God.

Throughout 2 Corinthians Paul has been wrestling with this issue. The super-apostles have invaded the Corinthians church with a gospel of success. If you are successful, they argue, then you are right and God is blessing you. And they made themselves exhibit A. But these super-apostles were false apostles who preached ANOTHER JESUS, a Christ without the cross; they preached another gospel which kept Palm Sunday and Easter, but erased all that happened in between. In contrast, Paul offered the church a Christ who WAS CRUCIFIED IN WEAKNESS, BUT LIVES BY THE POWER OF GOD. The same is true for us who live in Christ: WE ARE WEAK IN HIM, but at the same time WE SHALL LIVE WITH HIM BY THE POWER OF GOD (13:4).

The true, first, and final issue for God's people is not success and failure but faithfulness. EXAMINE YOURSELVES TO SEE WHETHER YOU ARE HOLDING TO YOUR FAITH (v. 5). We will succeed and we will fail, but true success and failure is hid in the mystery of the cross, God's power in weakness. So the real issue is faithfulness. Paul prays for his church that YOU MAY DO WHAT IS RIGHT, THOUGH WE MAY SEEM TO HAVE FAILED (v. 6). Paul can be glad in every success of the church, but he also is glad in his weakness.

It should be no surprise that Paul and Corinth are struggling with these issues, or that the American church struggles still. Given the runaway success orientation of our culture, and our addiction to immediate results whether in drugs or religion or business—we want *quick fixes* in every sense of the word—the church is tempted to hop, skip, and jump from Palm Sunday's triumphal entry to Easter's trumpets and bypass the agony of Gethsemane and the horror of the cross.

Holy Week, if we pay close enough attention, teaches us the defeat which is victory and the failure which is success.

II

"The Magnificent Defeat": the phrase is Frederick Buechner's in his sermon on Jacob. It describes what happened in the wrestling at the river Jabbok, where Jacob emerged wounded but transfigured, his hip wrenched out of socket, defeated yet somehow also victor, formerly Jacob now Israel, and limping toward the dawn which is the face of God.[1]

But the irony of victory in defeat is nowhere more staggeringly present than in the week we walk with Jesus from Palm Sunday to Easter. The hosannas of Palm Sunday soon to turn to the curses of crucify Him, last supper farewells no one understands, disciples turned into traitors, the horror of a cross, then the impossible triumph of Easter. No week of history could better embody the phrase, "The Magnificent Defeat."

Jesus entered Jerusalem amid the cheers and hosannas of the crowd, but Jesus was not fooled by this hurrah, he was not seduced by this superficial success. Hours later he would weep over Jerusalem, for he saw the rejection hidden behind the surface of their cheers. These people wanted only a Messiah garlanded in success. A suffering Messiah was beyond their believing.

Jesus had many opportunities to turn that Passover week in Jerusalem into a political, military success like the world had never seen. Patriotic and religious fervor was never higher for the Jews than during Passover. Hatred toward Rome, the occupying superpower, was at fever pitch. And it was a short step from Caesar to Pharaoh and from Exodus to revolt. "King Jesus, son of David, could make our country great again! He will set us free from Caesar!"

There were any number of times Jesus could have begun the revolt. At the triumphal entry into Jerusalem with the crowd waving palms and shouting hosannas, but Jesus rode a lowly donkey not a hero's stallion. Or at the scourging of the Temple when he upset the tables and drove the money changers out, but as he drove them out Jesus said, "My house shall become a house of prayer for all peoples." He did not say, "This house shall be the headquarters for holy war against Rome." Or, on the night when he was arrested and Judas betrayed him with a kiss and the soldiers came to arrest him, a disciple rushed to Jesus' rescue and cut off the ear of the high priest's slave. But Jesus said, Stop, put your sword away; all who live by the sword, die by it. Then he healed the ear of the enemy.

Then on the cross itself the soldiers tormented him and taunted him to call on God's angels and come down from the cross. And in Jesus' ear echoed the temptation of Satan in the wilderness, "If you are the son of God, throw yourself down from here; for it is written, 'He will give his angels charge of you to guard you'" (Luke 4:9-10). What a great moment to call down the legions of angels, rescue himself and start a holy war. But Jesus knew the failure which was the final success and prayed, Father, forgive them.

III

Jesus teaches us in Holy Week how to fail. He had earlier given his disciples what John Oman called "the forgotten sacrament,"[2] that is, the shaking off the dust, which is a "sacrament of failure."

Jesus gave his disciples four great symbols, three of which we use often in our common life. The washing of water, baptism, sign of repentence and forgiveness; bread and cup, the Lord's Supper, a sign of the intimacy of the family of God; and the laying on of hands, sign of the gift of the Holy Spirit we need in the practice of our ministry. But there is another, the "forgotten sacrament," shaking the dust off our shoes.

In his wisdom and mercy, Jesus prepared us for the hardest reality of our ministry, when our ministry is rejected, when we are unable to minister any more. He knew that our hope in the gospel and our love for people would create a danger: that we would be unable to handle or to admit our failure in ministry. Jesus knew we would meet opposition. Some people would not welcome us and there would be no way we could bless them with God's blessing. He knew we would run hard against the limits of our existence, our limits, others' limits. There are limits in people's willingness to hear the gospel, and there are limits in our own ability to minister.

So he gave us a sacrament of failure, the shaking off of the dust (Matt. 10:11 *ff.*). When you go to a house or to a city with the gospel and they refuse to receive you and to welcome your gospel, shake the dust off your feet and move on. Do not beat on that door forever, do not change your message so they will accept you. Shake the dust and move on.

The shaking off of the dust is a sacrament of failure for it recognizes that *there are limits to our ministry beyond which we should not strain.* It was a freeing moment in his ministry, Carlyle Marney said, when he realized that he didn't have to be a blessing to everyone! We can try too hard.

This symbol puts responsibility where it belongs. We are responsible to be a witness to the gospel, but we are not responsible for the results—that is the hearer's responsibility. If people spurn us and our message, we are to shake off the dust and leave them to the grace of God and to the judgment of their own choices.

Sometimes the most crucial and redemptive thing we can do is to help people hear the *no* they are saying in their hearts and with their lives. The shaking off of the dust mirrors back to them their *no* and may be the only possible prelude to their saying *yes.* We must let people say *no,* echo it back so they can hear what they are actually saying, and, hopefully, turn. An analogy: parents have a responsibility to love, but there is a point where they must let their children loose and let them take responsibility for their choices. Love that refuses to allow any distance will destroy both parent and child.

As for us ministers of the gospel, if the door of opportunity is closed to us we are called to go on to other places and people. And we go with peace, knowing our failure is not God's failure, trusting God to send others to them and seeking ourselves new persons to touch with the gospel. The application also applies to the business world. We must know when to let go of a failure and move on. To romanticize a venture, to deny the possibility of failure, courts disaster. So in all areas of life, not just ministry, we need a sacrament of failure.

But this sacrament of failure means more. *It reminds us that there are some methods by which the kingdom of God is not to be advanced.*[3] It is a *renunciation of all methods inconsistent with the gospel itself.* When we sense our failure or are afraid of our failure, we are tempted to adopt methods unworthy of the gospel.

Sometimes we are tempted to water down the gospel and change it to fit the prevailing mood of the times. Hence we become HUCKSTERS OF THE GOSPEL, hawking it like cheap wine. We promise people health and wealth and success—far more than Jesus promised—and conform the gospel to our culture of narcissism. Or we may coerce people with guilt or threaten God's fury in order to induce results. Or we can be so consumed with institutional success that we are afraid to take the risks of the gospel in our world. Afraid of failure, we adopt the religion of "Don't Rock the Boat."

Or, we are tempted to use coercive political power to succeed. But the kingdom cannot be advanced that way.

Or we can seek the partnership of the state in the advancement of our religion. But the power of the state corrupts and undercuts true religion. Baptists have always held to the principle of *voluntarism* in religion. Any faith that is not voluntary is not true faith. To court the favor of the state, the protection of the state, the power and wealth of the state in order to build the church is to adopt methods unworthy of the gospel. Better to fail. German baptists now have publicly repented their support of Hitler. They accepted the protection of the state in exchange for their silence, and their freedom.

Or, we can equate America with the kingdom of God, and turn a worthy patriotism into an unworthy nationalism, justifying all sorts of things in the name of God. Jesus told his disciples to put down the sword. And he said at his trial, If my kingdom were of this world, my disciples would be fighting (John 18:36). You can't kill for Jesus, lie and cheat for Jesus. You can't buy or bully a soul into believing.

The sacrament of failure renounces all methods inconsistent with the gospel. The gospel depends on the fragile witness of love. John Oman, a British Presbyterian but sounding like a baptist, says,

> God has made in every heart a sanctuary into which only the persuasion of love has a right to enter, a sanctuary into which He Himself will not, with any other means, force an entrance. In view of this great fact, the Church should learn from her Lord how to fail, how to make failure her last and greatest appeal, how to fail, not in discouragement, much less in indifference, but in faith and hope and love.[4]

Paul is prepared to fail if that is what faithfulness brings (though he hopes not, 13:6). Jesus chose to succeed or fail in the fragile method of preaching to human hearts (the folly of preaching!), renouncing all coercion, trusting in the patient persuasion of a love that will not let us go. He would not coerce faith by supernatural gimmicks. He would not court the powers of religion or state. Jesus offered love in the form of a life given and let us be free to respond.

And we chose the cross for him. The cross is the final sacrament of failure. It mirrors the *no* we shout to Jesus and pound into his hands and shove into his side. It faces us with all the ways we reject him. "Were you there when they crucified my Lord?" Sure, we were all there. But at the same time the cross that mirrors our *no* turns transparent and we no longer see our *no* but glimpse the *yes* of God, seeing in his face an inconceivable mercy. The cross not only mirrors our "Crucify Him," but also reveals Jesus' "Father, forgive."

What does the apostle say, looking at the cross? "While we were still *weak* . . . Christ died for the *ungodly*. . . . While we were yet *sinners* Christ died for *us*. . . . While we were *enemies* we were reconciled to God by the death of his Son" (Rom. 5:6-10, author's italics).

And we weak, ungodly, sinners, enemies all, saying our *no,* living our *no* and dying in our *no,* saw him die for us and, miracle of miracles, we turned and said, *yes*.

All because Jesus *chose the failure which was victory* and bore in his broken body the sign of the magnificent defeat. He could have won, and we lost, but he lost—that we and all the world might win.

Notes

1. Frederick Buechner, *The Magnificent Defeat* (New York: The Seabury Press, 1966), p. 10.
2. John Oman, *Vision and Authority* (London: Hodder and Stoughton, 1928), pp. 308 *ff.*
3. Ibid., p. 311.
4. Ibid., p. 313.

24

Final Appeal

(13:11-13)

and Benediction

(13:4)

Paul closes with a final plea. It is a pastoral plea appropriate for every church, not just that fractious, fickle church Paul loved so.

FINALLY, he says as he leaves them with a string of single word imperatives, REJOICE: the Greek *chairete* can be used as a greeting, "hail" or "hello" or as a farewell, "good-bye" or "God be with you." Sometimes, then, this word is translated "farewell." But literally it means REJOICE. Paul is calling them to the one activity which unites us, doxology, to praise and thanksgiving in the Lord. Hearts filled with gratitude have no room for meaner spirits.

MEND YOUR WAYS: or it can be translated, "be restored by God." Both translations reasonate with his plea (5:20) BE YE RECONCILED, to God and to one another.

HEED MY APPEALS: a reminder not to forget what the letter has been trying to say.

AGREE WITH ONE ANOTHER: literally, be of the same mind, which is "the mind of Christ" who though he was equal with God emptied himself and took on the form of a servant (Phil. 2:5).

LIVE IN PEACE: As we do, the "God of love and peace will be with you" (v. 11).

GREET ONE ANOTHER WITH A HOLY KISS (v. 12). This could have been the kiss of greeting or the kiss of peace offered as part of worship.[1]

And as you do all these things, Paul adds, ALL THE SAINTS GREET YOU (v. 13).

Benediction: The Blessing of God

Paul closes—as God's ministers should close every worship and
every meeting in the Lord—with a benediction which is the blessing of God.

Such a blessing prays for God's continuing blessings as we part.
It says, As I leave you I leave with you something far better than I:
the abiding Spirit of God. Jesus said at his farewell address, "It is
to your advantage that I go away" (John 16:7). Our hearts beg to
differ; Lord, how could that be? Jesus answers, "For if I do not go
away, the Counselor will not come to you" (v. 7). Jesus knew that
his own ministry was limited by the physical constraints of his
earthly existence. God's Christ was both hidden and revealed in
the earthly body of Nazareth's Jesus. But as he left this world in
the flesh, God would send his Spirit, another Paraclete like Jesus,
only this Spirit would not be bound by time and space nor hid in
any peculiar humanness.

If this can be true for Jesus Christ, how much more for us ministers! We need to leave every worship and every encounter with
the offering of a blessing that God's Spirit will be with the people
in an even more real way than is possible through our human relationships. Every minister of Christ is a vessel of Christ's Spirit,
but a cracked earthen vessel. We are a window open to God, but it
is a flawed piece of glass people see through, sometimes distorting
his face. We are at the same time an open book and a closed door,
at the same time a highway for our Lord and a stumbling block to
him. How wonderful, then, that we can leave people with something far greater than we can give.

So Paul closes with these wondrous words of benediction:

THE GRACE OF OUR LORD JESUS CHRIST: grace as pardon and grace as power, healing grace and, when we are left un-
healed, sustaining grace, in all and every circumstance, grace
sufficient.

THE LOVE OF GOD THE FATHER: here is love, that while
we were still sinners, weak, ungodly, enemies of God, Christ died
for us.

AND THE FELLOWSHIP [*koinonia,* companionship] OF
THE HOLY SPIRIT: the companionship of the Spirit of God as
Paraclete, literally, the one called alongside.

BE WITH YOU ALL. Yes, you!

AMEN. So let it be. And in Christ we utter back our *amen!*

Note

1. Furnish, p. 582.

Coda:
A Tale of Two Cathedrals

Sometimes a symphony ends with a coda, a musically distinct piece which forms a proper closing to the work. As a coda, I offer you "A Tale of Two Cathedrals," a painful and wondrous manifestation of Paul's gospel of *strength in weakness*.

If I were to choose a piece of music to go with it, it would be Samuel Barber's *Adagio for Strings*. In fact, I listened to it play over and over as I wrote this piece. It is exquisitely painful and beautiful all at the same time, an adagio of suffering being transformed by love. How right that it was used as background music for two movies, *The Elephant Man*, the story of a hideously deformed British man who became a hero in his woundedness, and *Platoon*, the story of the tragic horror of Vietnam.

Here now is the story. It is a parable of life and ministry amid suffering and in the name and spirit of Jesus Christ, crucified Messiah and risen Lord.

A Tale of Two Cathedrals

It was the best of times, it was the worst of times, it was the age of wisdom, it was the age of foolishness, it was the epoch of belief, it was the epoch of incredulity, it was the season of Light, it was the season of Darkness, it was the spring of hope, it was the winter of despair.[1]

So began Charles Dickens in his famous classic *A Tale of Two Cities*. And if those words apply to two cities, London and Paris, during the French Revolution, they also apply to two cathedrals, Durham and Coventry, during World War II. This chapter is "A

Tale of Two Cathedrals," and between them lies the mystery of God's Providence.

The German Reich planned its blitzkrieg of England. Sites were picked out; Durham and Coventry were chosen to be bombed. Coventry was destroyed and Durham was saved, but that is just part of the story.

I

Durham Cathedral is one of the great old cathedrals of England. This masterpiece of Romanesque architecture sits on a stone cliff and just below, at its feet, the River Wear does a hairpin turn. From the riverbank, the cathedral juts stunningly up into the sky. In 1072, William the Conqueror had claimed the land and built a castle there. A hundred or so years later the cathedral was built on that same spot.

In *Godric,* Frederick Buechner's novel of the twelfth-century saint, Godric travels to Durham Cathedral soon after its completion. See it through his eyes:

> Even the flames of many candles can't light up this awesome dark, nor all the gathered throng of priests and monks and lords and common folk fill up this emptiness. The hooded monks chant Psalms and we wind slowly down, but all their voices raised at once are but the rustle of the wind through trees, the call of owls, in this vast wood of stone. The towns the Conqueror razed when he came harrying the north, the crops he burned, the beasts he felled, the Saxon folk he slew; all haunt these Norman shadows. The silence is the sum of all of their voices stilled. As long as these stones stand and this great roof keeps out the rain, Durham's cathedral will be dark with death.[2]

I walked in Godric's steps a few years ago and while it was dark with the death of ages, it was also deep with the mystery of God. Thick Romanesque columns support Norman vaulted ceilings, all of which wrap shadow and light in a universe of space carved and molded into the glory of God barely seen, and when seen wrapped in the shadow of mystery.

Built on the site of a fortress, the cathedral was described by Sir

Walter Scott as "half church of God, half castle against the Scot."
Somehow it has withstood the onslaught of both warrior and
weather to stand today much as it was built 800 years ago. It carries with it an air of invincibility.

Perhaps its most dramatic escape was during World War II. The
Nazi blitzkrieg flew over northern England. But when it ap-
proached Durham a mysterious mist, said to be sent by God, set-
tled over and around the town and concealed it from the bomber
pilots who flew above. "God saved the cathedral!" the people exclaimed in praise and joy. It stands as a sign of the providence of
God. There, perched on a cliff surrounded on three sides by the
River Wear, the cathedral seems to have lived a charmed existence, as if God has protected it with his hand. That is the tale of
one cathedral, Durham; now let's turn to another, Coventry.

II

Coventry's Cathedral did not escape the scourge of war. It too
was one of England's premier cathedrals. Begun in the thirteenth
century, it must have risen majestically over the England countryside. Over the years Coventry became a famous industrial town,
known in modern times for its manufacturing of cars and planes. It
was no wonder then that during World War II it became a chief
center for the production of instruments of war and as such became a prime target for German war planes.

On November 14, 1940, Coventry Cathedral died in the flames
which destroyed the city around it. No mist covered the city that
day. It was the first attempt ever made in warfare to destroy a city
in one single operation from the air. It was a devastating technique
used many times thereafter, but Coventry was first and a new
word came into the language, *coventrate*, which means to destroy
utterly. That the bombs did. The cathedral, along with the city,
was utterly destroyed. It is hard for the mind to grasp the horror of
that day with human bodies lying wasted all through the town.

The city had the choice of how to respond to the devastation:
whether to take the road of vengeance and hatred or the road of
forgiveness and renewal. It is the choice we, all of us, have when

life has done its worst to us. At that moment of choice, in C. S. Lewis' words, "The Angels of God hold their breath to see which way we will choose to go."

The angels held their breath that morning when the provost of the cathedral, Richard Howard, walked through the rubble with a small group from the church. Among them was Jock Forbes, a stonemason and caretaker of the cathedral grounds. Jock was unlearned in formal theology, but out of the instinct of the faith learned in his lifetime of being a Christian, he did a simple thing that will never be forgotten. Kicking around in the rubble he found two charred beams from the fourteenth-century roof, fastened them into the shape of a cross and planted that cross in a mound of rubble, thus transforming it into a Calvary. As if to underline the message, a local priest, A. P. Wale, fastened three nails into the form of a cross, nails which had fallen from the fourteenth-century roof and now littered the ground. The road was taken. The words of Christ spilled into the air, "Father, Forgive." Two months later, Forbes built a rough stone altar and placed it where the old altar had stood. There in the ruins the words "Father, Forgive" were inscribed. The charred cross was placed behind the altar and on the altar was the cross of nails. The place was to become a place of reconciliation.

A new cathedral was planned. The words from Scripture became prophecy for them: " 'The latter glory of this house will be greater than the former,' saith the Lord of hosts" (Hag. 2:9, NASB). Those words of Haggai to Coventry strike an uncanny resonance with Haggai's own setting. The people of Israel had believed their own Temple inviolable, perfectly protected by God, but war had destroyed both Jerusalem and the Temple and standing there in the ruins of history, they heard the Word of the Lord: "The latter glory of this house will be greater than the former."

Those words illuminate the latter glory of Coventry Cathedral. A new cathedral rose from the ashes of the old cathedral. As you approach the rough stone altar, you see the two charred roof beams fashioned into a cross. Inscribed there are the words "Father, Forgive." And on the altar there stands the cross of nails.

Only then do you turn to your left and see the entrance to the new cathedral. The whole front wall is fashioned with clear glass so that you can see from the ruins into the new cathedral and so that you, from inside the new cathedral, will always see the ruins. It is a dramatic symbol of the redemptive grace of God: from crucifixion comes forgiveness and from forgiveness comes resurrection.

The new cathedral was built by people and with gifts from all over the world. As a sign of reconciliation, a German crew came and stayed six months building the international center there and helping with the new construction.

Coventry displays the most astonishing collection of contemporary Christian art anywhere in the world. As you enter the new cathedral your attention is grasped by the magnificent and breathtaking baptismal window depicting the light of God breaking into the world. On both walls, as you walk toward the pulpit and altar, are New Testament sayings inscribed. Then as you stand before the altar your eyes gaze up to the world's largest tapestry, 79 by 39 feet, which dominates the cathedral. There on this glorious tapestry is the risen Christ enthroned in glory wearing a workman's apron, his nail-scarred hands raised in blessing.

Contemporary Christian art is displayed throughout, gifts from all over the world, from Czechslovakia to Cincinnati. There is a Czech cross begun by its maker while he was in a prison camp during the war. There is a sculpture called *The Plumbline and the City* from Christ Church, Cincinnati, Ohio, a stirring reminder of Amos's dream about the righteousness of God as a plumbline.

As you leave the cathedral, the inscription beneath the west window catches both eye and imagination:

> To the Glory of God
> This Cathedral Burnt
> November 14, A.D. 1940
> Is Now Rebuilt 1962

In the mystery of God's redeeming grace, it has all been to his glory. Pilgrims come from all over the globe to see the new cathedral and to be touched by its message of forgiveness and reconciliation. And there has arisen from the cathedral an organization

called the Community of the Cross of Nails, formed and devoted
to the ministry of reconciliation. Chapters of this Community of
the Cross of Nails have formed all over the world. Coventry has
attracted artists from all over the world and challenged them to put
God's vision into art. For example, Benjamin Brittain's religious
masterpiece *War Requiem* was first performed there.

" 'The latter glory of this house will be greater than the former,'
saith the Lord." Indeed.

It was the latter glory of which Jesus spoke when he said, "Destroy this temple, and in three days I will raise it up" (John 2:9),
meaning the temple of his body, the temple of the kingdom
founded on forgiveness and ending in resurrection glory.

Coventry Cathedral: there may be no more profoundly moving
place of worship in the world.

III

Have you forgotten about the other cathedral, Durham? Let's
go back to the morning after the bombing raids. Looking at Durham and Coventry what would you have said? God saved Durham,
but not Coventry? Would you have said that God's glory shone
brighter around Durham than Coventry?

The intervening years have given us deeper insight into the
mystery of God's Providence, and this tale of two cathedrals becomes a parable of His Providence.

There are those who seem to have lived a charmed existence
relatively free from the crippling blows of pain and darkness,
those for whom Durham is their tale; and there seems to be no
discernible pattern as to why. "He makes his sun rise on the evil
and on the good, and sends rain on the just and on the unjust"
(Matt. 5:45). These words of Jesus suggest that the providence of
God is the impartial goodness of God extended to good and evil
alike, which is to say that wherever God's providential care is at
work it is at work for everybody regardless of their moral status,
their ecclesiastical affiliation, or their political persuasion.

So the question comes: did God really send the mists to cover
Durham and, if so, why did he not send them to cover Coventry as
well? And I confess the perplexity is deep. It is difficult for me to

imagine a God sitting in the heavens directing weather patterns. Weather patterns are too capricious in their capacity to give and take life for me to make God the director of their daily activity—though I think at this point we need to observe their essential goodness as making possible human life on this planet; the mystery of their goodness outweighs the mystery of evil.

We can only say that God in His Providence would want no city bombed (as Jesus said, "It is not the will of my Father . . . that one of these little ones should perish," Matt. 18:14) and that he does all he can do within the preserving of our freedom as human persons to clear the clouds and mists of our minds and hearts to prevent such a thing.

But while I am reluctant to make God the sender of those mists over Durham, nevertheless, I give him thanks for them. Who of us could, or should, have stifled the impulse of gratitude in Durham that dramatic day of rescue? For any act of goodness or good fortune it is right to give thanks, though it is not right to claim special status with God as a reason.

But Providence is not to be seen only in cases like Durham, where people are miraculously rescued from danger. Providence is also, perhaps more profoundly, seen in the case when the Spirit of God redeems us in the midst of destruction and makes our latter glory greater than the former. And that is, of course, where Coventry comes in.

I imagine that for most of us Coventry is more our tale than Durham. The mists have not come and protected us from life's onslaughts. Sin and death have done their jobs—both from within and from without. So the tale of two cathedrals becomes a parable of life.

If Durham is your story, if life has been kind, do not be ashamed to raise your thanks to God. For God's sake and yours, do not feel guilty over life having been so good to you. God would only wish more could have had your good fortune.

But if Coventry is your story and you have been left to sift through the rubble and wreckage of your life, I pray that you will find there a couple of charred roof beams and fasten them into a cross. I pray that from the ashes there will come a resurrection.

I do not think it is too much to pray that the latter glory of your house be greater than the former, for that latter glory will be the grace of Jesus Christ.

He will bind your wounds and nurse you back to your feet. He will take broken bones and mend them. He will take your pain and turn it to compassion; he will take your fearful heart and give you courage; he will take your hurt and fashion it into a passion for peace. Your Coventry will become your calling.

He will help you face your darkness with the words of Scripture: "[They meant it for evil;] but God meant it for good" (Gen. 50:20). You may walk with a limp, but you will walk. As pilgrims to Coventry do, you will still walk through the ruins of the old cathedral to get into the new, your scars may always be tender, but your life will be renewed by the grace of God. And you will minister that grace to others.

That is the opportunity for you on the other side of the cross. That is the crossroad of the cross, the cross in the heart of God and the cross in your heart.

> It was the best of times, it was the worst of times, it was the age of wisdom, it was the age of foolishness, it was the epoch of belief, it was the epoch of incredulity, it was the season of Light, it was the season of Darkness, it was the spring of hope, it was the winter of despair.

Such is the mystery of life, such is the mystery of Durham and Coventry. Only the word of the cross can penetrate the darkness of that mystery. Will you receive the healing of that word and follow in that way?

The angels of God hold their breath.

Notes

1. Charles Dickens, *Tale of Two Cities* (New York: The World Syndicate Publishing Company, n.d.), p. 9.

2. Frederick Buechner, *Godric* (New York: Atheneum, 1980), pp. 123-124.